# STRONGER than the STRONG

## LOUISE MORRIS

AN OMF BOOK

# STRONGER THAN THE STRONG

© 1998 Overseas Missionary Fellowship (*formerly China Inland Mission*)
Published by OMF International (U.S.), 10 West Dry Creek Circle,
Littleton, CO 80120-4413.

*Published 1998*

OMF Books ISBN 981-3009-14-4
CLC ISBN 0-87508-496-6

OMF Books are distributed by:
OMF, 10 West Dry Creek Circle, Littleton, CO 80120, U.S.A.
OMF, 5759 Coopers Avenue, Mississauga, ON L4Z 1R9, Canada
OMF, Station Approach, Borough Green, Sevenoaks, Kent TN15 8BG, UK
and other OMF offices.

Christian Literature Crusade
PO Box 1449, Fort Washington, PA 19034, U.S.A.
and other CLC offices.

This special OMF Books edition is available worldwide through:

CHRISTIAN • LITERATURE • CRUSADE

# STRONGER THAN THE STRONG

# DEDICATION

*This book is dedicated to my husband,*
*Jim Morris, who always held me to God's*
*highest purpose, and to our children,*
*Linda, Kevin and Nathan,*
*who shared our lives among the Karen people.*
*Without their help this account*
*would not have happened.*

# THANKS

*I would like to express my appreciation*
*to the team that worked with us*
*to reach the Pwo Karen:*
*Mary Bevan and Gill Cockfield from the U.K.*
*helped the new church in Prosperity Fields and*
*nearby villages. Christa Weber and Beate*
*Kaupp, from Germany, lived in Striped Creek*
*and taught in surrounding villages.*
*Later Jeremy Young from Ireland and Rein and*
*Maaike De Bel from Holland carried on in*
*Striped Creek. Four couples, Heinz and*
*Christianne Mayer, Hans and Beatrice Bar, and*
*Ben and Ursula Brutsch from Switzerland, and*
*Peter and Diane McIvor from New Zealand,*
*developed the work in Sop Lan. Nancy Stephens*
*from Canada continued the Bible translation.*

*My deep appreciation and heartfelt thanks*
*go to Ron Wilson for his encouragement*
*and help in writing this book.*

# FOREWORD

For centuries Satan, "Mangkholai," has been a tyrant who has ruled viciously over the Pwo Karen. The Pwo have lived in fear—fear of spirits, fear of sickness, fear of crop failure, fear of death, fear of outsiders, fear of curses, and fear of fear. Faith in Jesus brought them a freedom like nothing else has.

*Stronger than the Strong* is the story of how the Pwo Karen (po-ka-`ren) people of northern Thailand were reached with the gospel. It is not the whole story, but the breakthrough and beginning of an indigenous, biblical church movement. It took time for God to demonstrate His power over demonic forces, and for a people movement to Christ to develop. It took time for us to get to know the Pwo Karen and for them to get to know us and begin to trust in God, not man, medicine, magic or religion.

The Pwo Karen are a small part of the larger ethnic group known as Karen. About 2,600,000 Karen live in Myanmar (Burma) and 380,000 Karen live in Thailand. The two largest groups of Karen are the Sgaw (sa-`gaw) and the Pwo (po). Sgaw Karen have responded to the gospel in large numbers, but the Pwo have proved more resistant.

*Stronger than the Strong* tells how Jesus overcame Satan and spirits. Demonic forces dominate the daily lives of the Pwo Karen. Over the years Jesus proved to be more powerful than the spirits, and able to set the Pwo Karen free from bondage and fear. The promise of Hebrews 2:14,15 became true for many Pwo Karen believers: "Since the children have flesh and blood, he, too, shared in their humanity so that by his death he might destroy him who holds the power of death—that is, the devil—and free those who all their lives were held in slavery by their fear of death." It was worth years of waiting for God to set free the captives of the tyrant. Jesus is truly stronger than the strong.

JIM MORRIS
September 1998

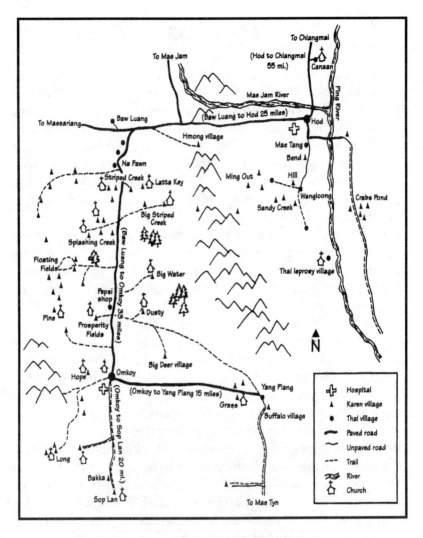

THE LAND OF THE PWO KAREN
NORTH THAILAND
1998

# PART I
# ON THE PLAINS
## 1959-69

*The first baptisms*

# 1

## GREAT EXPECTATIONS
### North Thailand, 1965

F lame trees with their scarlet blossoms lined the country road, filtering the tropical noon sun from the small group of people gathered at the edge of the flooded rice fields. The Big Day had arrived at last—the day we had prayed and worked and waited for so long. We stood on a dry grassy bank beside a pool that had backed up from the new dam on the Ping River. Fortunately it was December. The rice crop had already been harvested, so the high water hadn't damaged it. Beyond the fields and their green border of trees rose the mountains of North Thailand where the Pwo Karen tribal people lived. None, as far as we knew, were Christians; all worshiped spirits.

But today, five from that tribe who lived down on the plain, would take the important step of baptism. Some Christian Karen from Gong Loy, 40 miles away, had come for the first Karen Believers Conference. Teaching, feasting and fellowship were now culminating in this very special ceremony. Our field leader and his wife had driven 80 miles from Chiangmai to be with us. Karen families from our neighborhood crowded into his van to get a free three-mile ride to the baptism site. When no more could fit in, a slight quarrel arose over who had to pay five cents to take a local bus to the baptism site.

The ceremony began when my husband, Jim, and our co-worker, Ed, wrapped checkered sarong cloths about their waists, tied the long end up between their legs and tucked it into their belts. Carefully, with bare feet, they stepped into the thick black mud and waded out until the murky water reached their waists. The water felt cool in the hot sun. We sang, "I Have Decided to Follow Jesus," then Jim turned to the crowd and explained that the step these five people were taking was a public sign that they had turned from their old way of worshiping evil spirits and had decided to follow Jesus.

Boy Jee, a tall, lanky father of four, had never seen a baptism ceremony. He had been the first Karen to believe, so he was the first to be baptized. As he picked his way through the mud to where Jim and Ed stood, we remembered the long process that brought him to this crucial decision. He and his family lived next door to us in the Karen village of Sandy Creek near the Thai market of Wangloong. All day long they watched what we did. Their eight-year-old daughter, Gleck, and six-year-old daughter, Bee, in their long white dresses, stood in our doorway from early morning until late at night. Their only son, Kwae Poo, was the same age as our four-year-old Kevin. They made mud pies, compared shiny beetles, and rode tricycles. Their oldest daughter, Date Mung, a pretty teenager who recently cut her hair in bangs, helped us with the housework.

Boy Jee had never been to school. He owned no rice paddies but earned his living carrying heavy loads on his back across mountain trails to the Thai town of Omkoy. His wife stayed at home caring for the children. She spent many hours sitting on their bamboo porch with a hand loom belted to her waist and stretched out before her, weaving intricate patterns into their red shirts, bags and skirts. The family never grew tired of listening to the gospel records and stories about Jesus. "Jesus is stronger than the demons. He has power to deliver people from evil curses. He loves us and takes care of us." It was good news, but it was too hard for them to be the only Karen family to believe in Jesus. Other Karen would laugh at them and say they had left the Karen way and were following the foreigner's way. They would ostracize them from their village and refuse to share food or include them in village ceremonies. In their culture, such isolation could mean death.

A young man, Shway, from the Sgaw Karen tribe in Chiangrai, had come to help us. Shway spoke a different dialect, but felt he could learn the Pwo Karen dialect quickly if he lived with a Pwo family. Before long he moved into Boy Jee's house. While they taught him the local dialect, he taught them more about Jesus. He didn't find it easy to eat their rice-and-peppers diet—he was used to more fruit and vegetables—but it paid off. Late at night the kerosene lamp flickered as he sat on their porch playing his guitar, singing choruses, and answering questions, not only about Jesus, but about the strange white foreigners whose ways were so different. "If we become Christians can we still eat rice?" some wanted to know. "Do we have to drink milk?" "Can we still wear our Karen clothes if we believe in Jesus?"

A year later Boy Jee and his wife started coming to our house for Sunday meetings.

"Yes," they said, "We want to believe in Jesus." But they kept putting off the big decision. One day Mrs. Boy Jee's relatives needed to choose the new spirit head for their clan. All the family members were required to attend a special ceremony to inaugurate the oldest living woman as the new priestess, but they didn't invite Mrs. Boy Jee, because, they said, "She is a Christian; don't call her."

With that, Boy Jee decided to ride the fence no longer and told Jim, "Next Sunday I will really believe." But the next Sunday he had to carry a load of kerosene tins over the mountains, so the meetings came and went without Boy Jee. Would he remember? Or was he purposefully putting off the decision which would cut him off from other Karen people?

On Monday morning Jim ran an errand on his motorcycle. A few minutes after his return, Boy Jee came home and Jim reminded him, "Are you going to turn today?"

"Yes," Boy Jee replied. So after supper Jim, Shway, and the family gathered around the little wick lamp in Boy Jee's house. Jim explained how to pray to Jesus. "Just tell Him you are done with demon worship, ask His forgiveness, and tell God you are now going to follow Him." Boy Jee prayed by himself but his wife said, "I don't know what to say," so she repeated words of confession after Jim. Date Mung, their daughter, was too embarrassed to pray aloud. So Jim told her to "pray in your heart." After a few silent minutes, she said, "Okay, I'm finished."

Unity in Karen society is essential. It's almost impossible for a single person to make an individual decision. The nuclear family—everyone who sits around the meal tray or who sleeps around the fire—needs to make that decision together.

Now the Boy Jee family was ready to declare their new faith to the village, so they removed the dusty bamboo fetishes from their doorway and house posts. Date Mung brought a big field knife and Boy Jee cut off the grimy demon strings from their wrists and necks, while Jim and Shway prayed over each one. Finally they stoked the fire and burned the fetishes as we sang, "Into My Heart, Come Into My Heart, Lord Jesus." Precious prey, we knew, was being snatched from the Tyrant. It was all we had waited to see. Boy Jee stopped working on Sundays and opened his home for Sunday meetings. He began to learn to read. Jim took him on trips to other villages. Other people far and near heard that Boy Jee and his family had entered Jesus and were watching to see what drastic calamity would happen to them. And now, today, he was going to be baptized.

"Boy Jee, do you believe Christ died for you and rose again? Forsaking the demons, do you intend to follow Him always?" Boy Jee affirmed that he indeed trusted Christ and determined to follow Him in faith and obedience. Absolute silence fell on the crowd as Jim and Ed put their arms around him and lowered him into the water. As they brought him up dripping wet, a ripple of laughter and relief swept across the audience. Later Boy Jee explained, "I wondered what was going to happen to me. When you said that Jesus died, was buried three days and rose again, and that baptism was like dying with Christ and being raised to new life, I thought you might hold me under the water for three days." He had more faith than we realized. No wonder his family was relieved to see him rise immediately out of the water!

Boy Jee's wife was next. Hiking her red sarong higher and tighter around her waist, she stepped into the muddy water. A frightened frog jumped away. This time Jim asked Boy Jee to help him lower her into the water. She came up laughing, wiping her face with her hands.

Mr. Gawk was next. Mr. and Mrs. Gawk had lived near us in Sandy Creek. They, too, had heard the gospel records often and had watched how we lived. One day Mrs. Gawk appeared at our co-worker's door, "Come see my husband. He wants to believe in Jesus. I asked my mother (Headman Spider's wife) if I should let him believe, and she said, 'Yes, let him believe. I wanted your father to believe before he died, but he wouldn't listen to the missionaries.'"

Jim and Ed found Mr. Gawk lying on a thin, dirty mattress on the floor, so emaciated and sick he could hardly turn over to cough out the foul rusty sputum into a tin can by his mat.

"Can Jesus make me well?" he asked in a rasping voice.

What could we say? We taught the Bible stories that Jesus healed sick people. We believed in God's almighty power. But this man demanded an answer now!

"Yes, Jesus has power to make you well if it is His will. He is stronger than Satan and the spirits, but your inner heart is more important than your physical body, you know. It is more important that Jesus forgives your sins and makes your inner heart clean and gives you eternal life than to heal your body." But Gawk didn't seem to comprehend such a theological answer.

"I've wanted to believe in Jesus for a month, but my wife wouldn't let me. We have divined several times to see what sacrifices we needed to make to the spirits. We have used up all our pigs and have no money left. Spirits have failed; the Buddhist priests have failed; friends have failed. Only Jesus can help me now."

Ed warned him that we couldn't guarantee a cure, but he insisted that Jesus would heal him.

"We will have to take him to the hospital," we told his wife.

"Yes, take him. He is yours to do whatever you can for him."

"What if he dies along the way?"

"Do whatever you like. Chuck his body in the ditch; it doesn't matter to me. He is yours now," was her callous reply. She was fed up with the loss of her pigs and all this fuss.

Ed led him in a prayer and fed him some sweet milk. God must bring us very low sometimes before we are willing to call out for His help. But He who is able to save to the uttermost is only too willing to receive any who reach out to Him in a feeble flicker of faith. Would He heal Mr. Gawk?

A week later Jim took Mr. Gawk to the hospital in Chiangmai. "Oh, he's been here before and we sent him home to die," said the hospital receptionist. "We can't do anything more for him."

Jim had no place to take the sick man that night, so he pleaded, "Can't you keep him for just one night? Tomorrow I will come take him back home." They finally agreed and put Mr. Gawk in the terminal ward with three other dying cases.

The next morning Jim fasted and prayed before we went to see Mr. Gawk. When he entered the terminal ward Mr. Gawk's first words were, "Jo Dee (Jim's Karen name), have you ever seen Jesus? He was here standing beside my bed last night. He is going to make me well." One person in the ward had died. Normally Karen people are deathly afraid of a corpse and certainly would not remain in the same room with one, but Mr. Gawk wasn't afraid because Jesus stood beside him. The hospital staff said Mr. Gawk had improved so much they were willing to keep him longer.

The second day Jim visited Mr. Gawk was stronger, but

another patient had died, leaving an empty bed. The third day was the same. Mr. Gawk was improving, then another patient died, leaving a third bed empty. The fourth day Jim entered the ward and found all four beds empty, "Oh no, Gawk must have died, too," Jim thought. Then Mr Gawk walked out of the bathroom, looking better than ever. Flesh seemed to have grown on his wasted frame. In three weeks Mr. Gawk rode on the back of Jim's motorcycle back to the village. People were impressed at his quick recovery. "If you hadn't turned to God, you would be dead now," declared one neighbor.

Now at the baptism site Ed was asking, "Mrs. Gawk, do you renounce the demons and promise to follow Jesus's Way?" "Yes," Mrs. Gawk gave a hearty answer. Ed, with the help of her husband, lowered her into the water. When she came up she began scrubbing her arms, jangling and twisting her many brass bracelets. She undid her bun and rinsed her black hair in the water, then tossed it back and smoothed it into a knot in back of her head. Karen didn't often have that much water to bathe in, so she made the most of the situation.

Mrs. Pot was next. Mrs. Pot came to us as a thin, malnourished lady. Her husband was Gawk's son, an opium addict who spent most of the time in jail. Mrs. Pot lived with her in-laws, the Gawks, caring for her two small children who had the light hair and potbellies of starvation.

"Can I work for you so I can earn some money?" she asked.

"Well, do you think you have enough strength to carry water?" I replied doubtfully.

"I'll try."

Besides paying her to carry water, we gave her vitamins and bits of food. Day by day she looked better, grew stronger, and her children improved. She turned to the Lord and came to Sunday services. She quit smoking and carefully saved her hard-earned money until she had enough to pay for a little bamboo shack of her own. She moved out of her in-law's home and her smile grew wide as she recounted the many ways God had helped her. "My children are so much easier to care for since I entered Jesus."

"Mrs. Pot, do you promise to follow Jesus all your life?"

"Oh yes," she smiled timidly as Jim lowered her into the water.

Five Pwo Karen believers, the first fruits of the promised harvest. God had delivered each of them from a life of bondage to the spirits, and while they still had problems and much pressure from unbelieving Karen around them, each was a miracle of God's grace and mercy. We had worked in that village for six years but we had trained and studied and served for years before that. We hadn't despaired, but we often wondered how long it would take to see the gospel take hold in the life of a Pwo Karen. Now we hardly dared to voice it. Was this the breakthrough we had prayed for? Was this the fulfilling of the promise we believed God had given us that someday He would set the captives free?

Many months before Jim had told our colleagues that the Pwo Karen are like drugged prisoners of Satan. Our director had then given us this promise from Isaiah: "Can prey be taken from the mighty man, or can captives of a tyrant be rescued." The answer was clear. "Surely," says the Lord, "Even the captives of the mighty man will be taken away and the prey of the tyrant will be rescued. For I will contend with the one who contends with you and I will save your children." We could count on this. And here in front of us was the answer. I looked into the hazy distance at the mountains and thought of the thousands of Pwo Karen who lived there, and I wondered "How is God going to fulfill that promise for them?"

# 2
## EARLY FOUNDATIONS
### 1933-1957

That God chose me to be his child and serve him in Asia will never cease to amaze me. Yet, looking back I can trace his loving hand, guiding the circumstances that prepared me for work among tribal people. I was born during the Great Depression—not a convenient season—the first of seven children. I inherited the pioneer spirit from my parents who left all they had in Los Angeles and bought a few acres in the backwoods of Oregon. The place had some timber, a little farmland, creeks for running water and an old turkey house without electricity. That was our first home.

My grandmother, who traveled with us to the Northwest, read me stories from her missionary magazine. Grandpa led us in daily Bible readings and prayer. My parents took me to an evangelistic meeting where I heard about the two ways—mine and God's. My eternal destiny rested in that choice. As we stood to sing the closing hymn, the lady sharing my hymnbook slammed it shut and marched forward to indicate her decision to follow God. I knew I should have done the same.

Three years later, when I was eleven, I went forward at the Easter service while the congregation sang, "Give Me Thy

Heart." My family was surprised but glad. At the dinner table we joined hands as Dad led us in singing, "Blest Be The Tie That Binds Our Hearts In Christian Love."

When I graduated from high school I applied to Prairie Bible Institute in Canada. I thought perhaps a year of Bible study might be good before I went on to nurse's training. To my surprise, God had been speaking to my parents about going into full-time Christian work. Mother had seen an advertisement in the Prairie magazine asking for music teachers. With her college degree in music, she felt this was a great opportunity to use her talent for the Lord's work. But what would Dad do? Farming had been tough, but recently he had acquired a plumbing license. For the first time we had a better car and some extra money to improve the house, and he had just finished building a new home for my grandparents, who had lived in a one-room cabin next to ours.

Again that pioneer spirit emerged and fused with a desire to serve God. Dad, too, felt God was leading him go to Prairie Bible Institute. He agreed to study half time and do plumbing for the school half time. As a family, we packed up all five kids, waved goodbye to my two aunts and grandparents and drove up to Alberta, Canada, where the school was located. North of the border the paved highway became a gravel road. I thought this must be the end of the world. Finally, after three days of travel, we arrived to see a cluster of dull gray buildings huddled on the barren wind-swept land. This was Prairie Bible Institute, and I had no idea what God would do for me there. The year was 1950.

That first night I knelt by my bed and prayed, "Dear God, I don't know if I'm saved, but if I'm not, please save me now." And that was how I began four intensive years of the study of God's Word, study that changed me from deep inside and built a solid foundation for the rest of my life.

Prairie, I soon learned, existed for missions. Missionaries from all over the world streamed through chapel and classes, telling stories of cannibals in New Guinea and persecution in

South America. Some had fled from communists in China; others told of opportunities in Japan after World War II. They challenged us with reports of people in remote places of the world who hadn't heard about Jesus. Did God want me to be a missionary? I was young and healthy and couldn't think of any reason why I shouldn't go. So then I began to wonder where God wanted me to serve—Europe, South America, Africa? There were so many places. How could I know which was right for me?

A former missionary invited me to a prayer meeting for Asia where I learned there were fewer missionaries per population in Southeast Asia than anywhere in the world. I began reading books written by Isobel Kuhn. She had worked among tribal people who lived in flimsy bamboo shacks perched on the sides of deep gorges in China, and she made those people come alive. How wonderful it would be to teach the Bible to people who had never heard about Jesus and see them change from worshiping evil spirits to knowing the true and living God!

I didn't want to go to the mission field alone, however, but when my friend, Laurie, advised me to ask God for a man to be my spiritual leader, I countered, "Really? In this place?" Prairie had strict rules to keep boys and girls apart. When those rules seemed unreasonable, Laurie encouraged me, "Don't let frustration with a few rules rob you of blessings God has for you here." At the same time I noticed that in spite of the rules many young couples managed to get together.

One night my brother Stu told me, "Louise, a guy here at school is interested in you."

"Really!" I feigned disinterest, but I couldn't fool Stu. For a long time Stu wouldn't tell me his name, but finally he blurted it out: "Jim Morris."

I didn't know this Jim Morris, but I was curious. I had a dozen questions, and I hounded Stu for more information. I learned that Jim was from Kansas, liked to play basketball, had good grades and was a year behind me in school, even though he was three months older. So far so good! But was he interested in missions? If so, where? Stu didn't know, and we weren't allowed to talk to each other, so I had nothing to do but wait.

Little by little I learned more about the man God had chosen for me. Jim, too, came from a Christian home. His mother, Amelia, small and feisty, had married Clarence, tall and lanky, who worked 45 years for an oil company in Kansas City. Jim learned from his Dad's example to work long and hard for what you want and proved it by mowing lawns to earn enough money to buy his first bike. He grew up playing ball in the back lot and loving sports.

Jim worked on a farm one summer. One day, out of the blue, the farmer's son invited him to a Youth for Christ meeting at a camp in Indiana. A quick decision to go changed Jim's life. That week he walked down the sawdust-strewn aisle and gave his life to Christ. He was fifteen years old when he chose the Bible verses, Philippians 1:20,21 as the foundation for his life. "According to my earnest expectation and my hope" he repeated over and over again, "that in nothing I shall be ashamed, but that with all boldness, as always, so now also Christ shall be magnified in my body, whether it be by life or by death. For to me to live is Christ, and to die is gain."

When Jim tried out for basketball in high school the coach told him, "We already have a water boy." But Jim's small size didn't keep him from taking an open stand for Christ in high school. He joined a Bible club and carried his Bible with his school books. He joined a quiz team that competed with other high school Bible clubs. To do well the students memorized the entire book of the Bible on which they were being quizzed. God's powerful Word soon saturated Jim's quick mind and penetrated his heart. He preached his first sermon when he was sixteen, and before he left high school he knew that God wanted him to be a missionary. "Prairie's the place to prepare for missions," he was told, so he headed 2,000 miles from Kansas City to Prairie. Prairie's motto was "Training disciplined soldiers for Christ," and the principal challenged us to go where Christ has never been named and "carve out a kingdom for God."

Jim wasn't too small to play basketball at Prairie, however, and after school and on Saturdays you could find him in the gym. When the Prairie team won the local tournament, the coach invited them to his home to celebrate. The coach just happened to be my dad, and I just happened to be there helping mother.

The next year Jim made friends with my brother Stu, and, because he played in the trumpet trio, he had a good excuse to make an occasional visit to the music department where I worked.

One day he asked to borrow my typewriter, and when I handed it to him, his hand closed over mine. I looked up and saw his intense eyes looking right through me, and knew this was serious business. For graduation he gave me a Bible in which he had written, "Dearest Louise, May our lives ever be centered upon the firm foundation of God's Word until with Job we cry, 'I have esteemed the words of His mouth more than my necessary food.' (Job 23:12). May our desire be to teach this Word in the regions beyond. In His Precious Name, with love, Jim." Jim was strong, athletic and fun, but more than that, he was a man I could respect and one who would be my spiritual leader. Going with him would mean a life of obedience to God and obviously would involve missions. Later I learned he, too, had read books by Isobel Kuhn and was open to going to Southeast Asia.

From the Scriptures I received the assurance that "this is the Lord's doing; it is marvelous in our eyes," but what would Dad say? He always maintained that you get to know a person well on the basketball court. Does he play fairly? Is he a good sport? Is he a team player? Dad knew Jim from many basketball games, and told me firmly, "There's no one else I'd rather see you marry than Jim Morris."

That settled the question for me, but not the timing. We

became engaged and began correspondence with OMF, and they replied: "Get married and get your training and then apply to the mission." We were delighted and began making wedding plans. About that time, J.O. Sanders, the highly respected director of OMF, came to speak at Prairie. Many students signed up to speak with him, but we already had the word from OMF and didn't think we needed an interview. He asked to see us, however, and gave us very different advice than we wanted to hear: "Wait until you are on the field two years before you get married." Our hearts sank. Did we mean business with God? Was God really calling us to tribal work in Southeast Asia? How long would it be before we could get married? If we took more training and then another two years on the field, we were looking at seven years of waiting at least. Many questions arose in our minds. We decided to think it over for a year.

That year I took a course in missionary medicine at Biola while Jim worked for Canadian Sunday School Mission in British Columbia. Jim felt tempted when the director asked him to stay on and lead the work. Did God want him to leave this fruitful work with so much yet to be done? But his vision for overseas still burned.

Letters flew back and forth as we agonized. Should we follow the mission director's advice or get married? We seemed to get no clear leading—just the same question over and over. At last we decided to take the safe way, forget further training and go to the field. If God didn't want us to go he would stop us. Deeply disappointed, I packed away my wedding things, and that October we attended candidate school in Philadelphia.

I confess I was surprised when we were accepted into OMF. I certainly was a reluctant candidate. After years of committing my life to go wherever God led, I had second thoughts. This was real. This was leaving home. I wished something would happen to stop me—I'd break a leg, catch some disease or learn that the mission had made a mistake—anything to prevent us from getting on that boat. But nothing stopped us. Instead the way opened widely before us. In March 1957 we boarded a Dutch liner for England to join other prospective missionaries bound eventually for Singapore and then for fields of service all over Asia. We still had much to learn of God's way of teaching patience.

# 3

## PEOPLE WHO SIT IN DARKNESS
### 1957-59

Jim rolled over on the foam pad and pulled the white cotton blanket tighter around his neck. The swaying motion of the train had jerked him awake. "Where am I?" he thought, then remembered, "We must be getting close to Chiangmai." He threw off the blanket, pulled back the heavy curtain, and peered out to see a wall of thick green bamboo jungle plunging down the mountain side into a deep ravine. North Thailand was quite a change from the flat rice fields in Central Thailand where he had boarded the night before.

The train threaded a tunnel, emerged, and lurched to a stop at a tiny mountain station. Thai vendors thronged to the window holding up trays of roasted chicken legs and packets of white glutinous rice. Children ran along the track selling yellow and purple orchid plants they had gathered from the jungle.

As the train chugged on, Jim breathed in the cool mountain air. "Louise would love it," he thought. For eighteen months, Jim had studied Thai in the northern town of Chiangrai while I studied Thai in the southern town of Tak. During this time we had both visited various tribes in North Thailand. Each tribe was different. For a month I lived with a young family working among the Hmong people. The Blue Hmong wear blue short pleated skirts, while the White Hmong wear long narrow aprons over black trousers. Their outfits are lavishly trimmed with cross stitch. Akha people wear elaborate helmets trimmed with silver coins and dyed monkey fur. Jim lived with a missionary family in a Mien village. The Mien wear fancy embroidered trousers, with a red ruff trim on their black blouse. The Lisu wear big turbans, and the Shan dress like the Thai. Each tribe speaks a different language, and all worship spirits, except the Shan, who mix spirit worship with Buddhism. All these tribes needed more workers, and we wondered where the mission would send us.

Finally, the Field Council decided we should go to the Pwo Karen tribe. The term Karen covers a large group of people in Thailand and Burma who are divided into three main groups. The Sgaw Karen are the largest and have been responsive to the gospel. The Pwo, a smaller group, were much more resistant to the gospel. Several million Pwo Karen lived in Burma, which was closed to missionaries, but some 50,000 lived in Thailand along the Thai-Burma border.

The Pwo in Thailand had no Christians, no Bibles, no churches, no written language among them. An OMF couple, Orville and Hazel Carlson, had gone to live in Wangloong, a Thai town located near Karen villages, but after nine months left to become field leader. Joe and Laura Cooke worked among the Pwo Karen for two years but had to return home because of bad health. Another couple, Ed and Norma Lee Hudspith were then working with the Pwo and were delighted when they heard we would join them as new co-workers. Now Jim was on his way to visit them in Wangloong.

Jim got off the train in Chiangmai, swung his backpack over his shoulder, and made his way to the front of the station. Pedicab and taxi drivers pressed him, clamoring to be hired. "Hey, Mister! Come to me!" Jim picked a lean brown man with strong arm and leg muscles showing beyond his blue shirt and shorts. "Do you know the OMF home?" he asked in his best Thai. "Sure! 20 baht." Jim haggled the driver down to 10 baht, hopped into the buggy, a kind of three-wheeled bicycle with a carriage in back, and the man peddled away.

Fellow workers gave him a warm welcome, fed him breakfast and put him on a lumbering rice truck headed for Wangloong. After six dusty hours, bumping over 60 miles of gravel road, the truck stopped in front of the Hudspiths' home. Ed and Norma Lee came out to meet Jim with beaming smiles and helped him lift his backpack into the house. While Norma Lee handed him a cold drink, Ed began telling Jim about the area.

Wangloong was a thriving Thai market. Most of the Thai people made a prosperous living from illegal businesses. What interested Jim was that this was the main shopping center for many Pwo Karen who lived in twelve villages on the plains within an hour's walk of the market. They wouldn't live in the town itself, but kept their own culture, their own language and their distinctive red dress. The only Karen who lived in town were those who had married a Thai person and had, as the Karen put it, "taken a Thai heart."

Far beyond, in the tree-covered mountains surrounding Wangloong market, lay scores of Pwo Karen tribal villages. They had no roads, no hospitals, no schools, no phones, no electricity, no churches. All were animists—spirit worshippers—with a veneer of Buddhism, and if we wanted to reach them we'd have to trek over mountain trails to their villages several days away or contact them when they came into the market to buy salt or steel to make knives.

The next day Ed introduced Jim to two young Pwo Karen men, Abel and Louie, who gave Jim his first lesson in Karen language. Not used to sitting on a chair, Louie squirmed and fidgeted as Jim began asking him questions. "What's this?" Jim asked in Thai, pointing to a book.

"Jung," replied Louie, so Jim wrote it down.

"What's this?" Jim asked next, pointing to a chair.

"Jung," Louie answered again.

Hmm, Jim thought. The word can't mean both of those. Still he wrote it down and tried again, this time pointing to a table. When he got the same response, he began to work it out. He was pointing with his finger, and the Karen point with their noses. "Jung" he learned, was the word for finger. It was an early warning. Language learning would involve more than just words. We had to learn how these tribal folk think.

Ed told Jim how they tried to make gospel records, but the first time they had trouble finding the right word for "Lord Jesus." The word on the records was Yeashu, a term similar to the one used by Pwo in Burma. But in Thailand that word means 50 cents—only half a dollar—and is a slang term for "half-wit." The records were urging people to believe in Lord Half Wit instead of Lord Jesus! Ed quickly made a new set to correct the mistake. Jim began to see what a task he had before him.

Ed explained his plan to survey the Pwo Karen area. "We'll walk out to Maesariang and then south and circle back to Omkoy. We can see how many villages there are, and find out if anyone is interested in hearing more about Jesus." Jim agreed and they began to prepare. They hired a couple Karen men to be guides and carriers. Having Karen men with them meant Ed and Jim would be accepted more readily into strange villages. They stuffed sleeping bags into backpacks and threw in packets of soup, a couple of pans, a tea kettle to boil water, and some candy. They could buy rice along the way from the Karen, but mostly they'd rely on Karen hospitality to feed them. As a treat, Norma Lee baked a fruitcake to take along.

As soon as the rainy season ended they started off. The reception in the first village was cool. "You can't come here," the headman's wife told them. "Go to that village over there." She was scared of the two strange white men who suddenly appeared close to her porch. But the Karen carriers climbed up the ladder to the house and started explaining who we were. After a while Jim and Ed climbed up, too, and began playing

27

the gospel records. Soon a crowd gathered. "That box talks Karen language!" they exclaimed. Fear dissipated as they listened over and over to the records.

Then Ed showed them some big poster pictures: Creation, the lamb sacrifice, the flood, the tower of Babel, the birth of Jesus, His miracles and finally His death and resurrection. The pictures of men with long robes and beards was strange and so was the story these white men told. Was it really true that God loved them and that He is stronger than the demons? "You must stay here tonight," they begged. So Ed dug out his medicine box and began treating some sick people.

Jim couldn't speak much of the language yet, but he observed and had time to reflect. He felt as if he were walking around the walls of Jericho—great, thick walls of difficulty which only the mighty power of God can destroy. One wall was bondage to fear of evil spirits. The Pwo Karen were constantly afraid they might offend the spirits and have to appease them with pig and chicken sacrifices. Another was the wall of materialism. The Karen begged for his shirt, his watch, his flashlight—everything they could see. Many said they'd turn to Christ if he could guarantee them plenty of rice and freedom from sickness. That was their main interest.

Then there was the wall of vice. From little infants to old people, everyone smoked tobacco, drank whiskey, chewed betel nut, a mild narcotic, and smoked opium. And Jim was painfully aware of the barrier of language—not only different words, but the meaning of certain words. How could he ever express spiritual concepts to these people? They had no words for "holiness," "faith," "repentance" or "forgiveness."

Lastly there was the physical wall to cross. We would have to climb those beautiful, rugged mountains to reach remote villages nestled among valleys. Standing on top of one ridge Jim counted thirteen layers of mountain ranges.

Jim pulled out a little book, *The Prayer of Faith*, written by J.O. Fraser, missionary to the Lisu of China. Fraser, too, had faced walls of resistance, and had recorded: "Sunday, January

16. Not a single person at service in the morning ... the walls of Jericho fell down 'by faith.' Of all the instances of faith in Hebrews 11, this corresponds most nearly to my case. But not faith only was necessary; the wall fell down after it had been compassed about for seven days. Seven days' patience was required, and diligent compassing of the city every day—which seems to typify encompassing the situation by regular, systematic prayer. Here then we see God's way of success in our work, whatever it may be—a trinity of prayer, faith, and patience." Jim knew that all three—prayer, faith and patience—would be needed to win the Pwo to Jesus Christ.

Reaching the villages often meant traveling dangerous trails. In one place the trail led straight down to the river. Looking for a place to cross, Jim stepped down into the water and grabbed a nearby branch to steady himself. As he did, part of the branch slid off into the water and swam away. It was really a long snake.

When Ed finally opened the fruitcake Norma Lee had packed, it had gone moldy. It took them three weeks to circle 3,000 square miles. They visited 32 villages, 22 of them for the first time. But no one in any of those villages was interested in turning to Jesus. Not surprising, Jim mused. How would I feel if a turbaned Sikh in strange robes came to my door and told me I should believe in his god? Would I be interested? Probably not.

The trip also taught Jim a lot more about Karen beliefs. In the beginning, they believed, God gave them a book of wisdom to live by. While they had this book they lived well, but one day they left it out on a stump. It rained and the pigs ate it; then it passed through the pig's dung, where the chickens pecked at it. Now their book was gone. What should they do? The Trickster, Mangkholai, came to their rescue and assured them, "Don't worry. The wisdom of your book is now in the bones of the chickens and the gall of the pigs. Just sacrifice them to me, then look at their bones and I will tell you what to do."

Since then the Karen have worshiped spirits with sacrifices

of pigs and chickens. When they're sick, they go to the demon priest who divines by looking at the holes in the chicken's thigh bones or at dregs in the whiskey cup and tells them if they have to sacrifice a black pig or a white pig, a male or female or both, or a white chicken or a red chicken. They must follow every detail, exactly as the demon priest tells them. If they recover from their illness, they say he was a good priest. If they don't get well, they seek out another demon priest and repeat the process. Soon, however, all their pigs and chickens are gone.

In later years, one of our neighbors, a widow with many small children, had an enormous mother pig. One day the pig went out to the jungle to make a nest for her babies, but she returned to the village without having given birth. That broke a taboo, and the demon priest ordered the woman to walk the big pregnant pig, along with a male pig, to her demon clan priestess who lived in a village eighteen miles away. When they killed the mother pig, they found eleven baby pigs inside her. These pigs would have made our neighbor rich, but all had to be sacrificed. The poor woman never owned pigs again. Such is the bondage to spirits.

Sitting around the fire in the evenings with a cotton blanket draped over their shoulders, the old Karen men smoked their pipes and told many stories about the spirits they believed in. Ter Mung Khwae, for example, are the big guardian spirits.

"Are these guardian spirits good to you?" we asked.

"Sometimes they are and sometimes they're not," they answered.

In truth, we learned the spirits are capricious. But the Bible tells us the devil is a murderer and liar from the beginning. His intentions are destructive. Slowly he was depleting the Karen of all their pigs and chickens.

The oldest living woman in each clan becomes a priestess and conducts the sacrifice ceremonies for all those related by blood in her clan. She has a special knife and pot and bag to carry these things in that are used for the ceremony.

Then there are village spirits which must be appeased three

times each year. The demon priest of the village conducts these ceremonies. He prays to the spirits of the land and the spirits of the water before plowing the fields, just before the rice grain begins to head out, and at harvest time to ensure a good crop and a prosperous year.

When they prepare fields, the Karen Way requires them to sacrifice nearly 30 chickens for each field throughout the growing season. The Karen Way is all-important. It's a great sin to break the traditional way of their ancestors.

Animists believe everything is animated by spirits. The Karen believe spirits live in houses, fields, water, rice, buffalo, and trees. They all must be given sacrifices of food and kept happy lest they become angry and cause calamity to fall on the people. Often we saw offerings to spirits put out along the paths with bits of tobacco, thread and betel nut placed on a piece of old cloth. Besides spirits, Karen believe in taboos that cause calamities when broken, and curses that will kill other people. At funerals they burn miniature shapes of buffaloes and houses and bury coins and tools, believing that these things will be used by the dead person in the next world.

Then there are souls who live on a person. Karen believe they have 33 souls—one for various parts of the body with the main one behind the ear. These must all be appeased with an offering and tied in with strings around the wrists. If one of these souls leaves, the person becomes sick and must make another sacrifice to call back his soul. If someone dreams, his soul is actually doing the things he dreams about. If someone wakes him up from a deep sleep too quickly, the souls may not have had a chance to get back to the body in time, so they must be called back and tied in. All their lives Karen live in fear that the bad spirits might "bite" them—that is, make them sick or cause a bad accident. Parents threaten their children with, "If you're bad, the demons will bite you."

What do they think about God? The old Karen men say God made them, but then He went off and left them and has now forgotten them. God really doesn't have anything to do with their present lives. In fact, according to legends, God got angry and drunk and was seduced by the Trickster. And that cone-shaped mountain over there is where He dumped the ashes from His pipe.

One old Grandpa squatting beside the fire with his head wrapped in a dirty cloth turban, stuffed a wad of tobacco into his pipe and pulled his tunic down over his knees as he told this story: One day God was working on a boat. Along came a person who told him, "God, God, you must come home. Your child is sick."

"Oh, my child is sick? Too bad," God answered. "But I can get another child," and He kept on working.

Another person ran to Him saying, "God, God, your wife is sick. You must come home immediately."

"My wife is sick? Oh, too bad. But I can marry another wife," he answered, and resumed working.

Someone else came and said, "God, God, your mother is sick. You must return home immediately."

"My mother is sick? Well, I can't get another mother." So God left and has never come back.

Will God ever come back? One Karen legend tells about a father who left his small children at home on a high porch with a litter of baby pigs. A tiger came and jumped at the house posts trying to get the children. Finally the children threw down a baby pig, which pacified the tiger for a time. Then it started jumping and growling again for another pig. Karen explain that they keep making pig sacrifices until their "father" comes back.

All this we learned over the next few years. Meanwhile Jim longed to be able to tell them the Bible stories of God's holy character, His mercy and faithfulness as He dealt with His people Israel, His love and care as He talked to individuals, His power, might and wisdom. These, he knew, must replace the age-old legends until gradually their concept of God changed. But for now we had to finish Thai language study.

After Jim's visit, I took my turn to visit the Hudspiths in the village where we'd eventually live. Norma Lee taught me the basics of homemaking in a place where the nearest convenience store was 100 miles away. The most important lesson was to boil all drinking water and cool it. Little children walked down the street carrying trays of strange vegetables on their heads and selling them for a few baht, and I learned how to cook okra and long skinny eggplant. I learned what do to with jackfruit, how to cut up a pineapple, how to make a tin of tuna fish last two days and a can of cheese last one month. Norma Lee taught me how to buy meat and how to cook a slab of raw pork the butcher just hacked off the carcass and wrapped in a banana leaf. She taught me about duck eggs and green pumpkins and yard-long beans. I learned the various leaves and roots used for flavorings and how to cook cabbage or serve cucumbers a dozen different ways. We sifted weevils out of the flour and baked bread. We sewed curtains and made skirts for ourselves from  lengths of hand-woven Karen material.

On the exact day, two years after we arrived on the field, Jim and I were married in Chiangmai. A western wedding in Chiangmai was rare, and every expatriate, whether they knew us or not, attended the ceremony in Prince Royal Chapel. We did everything ourselves, decorated, made bouquets, prepared food. The night before, a storm blew out the electricity, so the homemade ice cream in the freezer melted. Moments before the ceremony a transformer blew out. A friend who agreed to tape the wedding service found someone to hold two wires together to give him enough power to make a tape, but we had no electric power to play the music tape for the reception. The fruitcake we had made and frosted and set on pillars collapsed.

But after the long wait to be married, these seemed to be minor troubles. With Thai students peering in through every door and window, we were finally married. We took a short honeymoon, then climbed aboard a ten-wheel rice truck for the seven-hour ride from Chiangmai to our first home in Wangloong.

# 4
## THE BEST CHRISTMAS PRESENT
### 1960

Wangloong was not our first choice of a place to live. We wanted to reach the Karen people, and we longed to live in a Karen village where we could mingle with them, but they wouldn't allow it. They said everyone inside their invisible village fence must worship demons. We didn't worship spirits, so we would break the village unity. Village unity is extremely important in Karen culture. Everyone must do the same thing, plant the same crop, and worship the same way. To deviate from the Karen Way is to break solidarity—which is a cardinal sin.

Wangloong market was the closest we could get to the Karen. Each day we opened our front doors and called to them as they passed along the street, "Where are you going?" They'd stop and stare at our strange white faces, but they didn't understand Thai. We needed to learn the Pwo Karen language.

Joe Cooke, a missionary before us, was gifted in linguistics and had worked out six basic lessons in Pwo. We started working on them, trying to discern the sing-song tones and figuring out the sounds and structures of this unwritten language. We spent hours getting Karen to tell us stories, recording these stories on tapes and then listening to them, transcribing them, searching for words to express location, time, emphasis, and grammar patterns that indicate where certain words should come in a sentence. We hired Abel and Louie, who spoke both Karen and Thai, to come study with us every morning. They became our close friends and told us much about their families. They were half brothers, having the same father, Demon Priest Monday, but different mothers.

Old Monday was famous for his skill in divination. When people were sick or some disaster happened, they thought the spirits were angry for some wrong they had committed and came to Old Monday for advice on how to appease them. He divined by examining dregs from a cup of whiskey or from the holes in the thigh bones of a chicken and he told them what sacrifice they had to make. They made that sacrifice hoping the spirits would make them well. For his services the Karen paid him enough to make a living.

Wangloong was one of the hottest and driest places in Thailand during the dry season and one of the hottest and steamiest places in the rainy seasons. We drank gallons of cold tea and still felt thirsty. For a while we tried to lay down for a short rest after lunch, but without a fan, all we did was soak our pillows with sweat, so we decided to use the afternoons to visit nearby Karen villages.

Abel and Louie invited us to their home in Hill Village, and introduced us to their family. They showed us how the Karen do things like pound rice, then sift out the chaff, and cook the kernels over the wood fire in their front room. They set up their looms and showed us how they weave their garments and bags. They explained why they tie strings around the wrists of their children. When a child had a fever or a bad dream, they offered a chicken, an egg or a banana—whatever the demon priest required—to the souls, chanted a prayer asking the souls to please return to the child, then tied the souls in with string.

They also watched to see how we did things. Sometimes they were confused, wondering what is western culture and what is the Christian way. Each morning after breakfast Jim and I sat on our verandah and had morning prayers. When I sat down, our cat always jumped up on my lap. At that time the Karen lady we hired to carry water brought us two big buckets to fill our tank and we became friends.

One day we asked her, "You've heard us talk about Jesus. Why don't you become a Christian?"

"Oh, I couldn't become a Christian," she protested.

"Why not?" we asked.

"Well, I don't have a cat." She figured the cat on my lap was part of the ritual of prayer.

Wanting to contact more Karen people, we began visiting other villages, but we got a cold reception. As we walked into Sandy Creek, the nearest village, we could cut the tense, foreboding atmosphere with a knife. Old Headman Spider was steeped in Karen ways and warned his people about us. His wife, bent over stirring her rice pot, looked like a witch with her hooked nose and gnarled face with a strange knob in the middle of her forehead. As we passed by she looked up and gave us a wide toothless grin. When we called to people sitting on their verandas, "Are you home?" they wouldn't answer or they'd turn around and go inside.

"Go away," complained one lady. "You smell like soap and make my head ache." Looking at her and others, we could see that soap had not become a part of Karen culture. Another woman sitting on her porch was very unfriendly until we offered her medicine for her malaria. When she recovered she was more friendly.

Finally on the trail we met a woman carrying a load of charcoal to sell in the market. "We'll buy your charcoal" we offered. She was one of the first to let us sit on her porch and play the records, and later we found she was an aunt to Abel and Louie.

In Ming Out village some people had never seen a white person. They screamed, grabbed their children and ran inside the house.

"Hello" we called, "don't be afraid. We have a box that speaks your language." Then we pulled out our record player and the people listened with astonishment. Curiosity overcame their fear as they gathered around to hear the words and songs.

"How did you get a man to stay inside that little box? What do you feed him?" they wanted to know. "That record speaks better Karen than you do," they told us. "But what a strange message: Jesus loves us? He is stronger than the spirits? We never heard such a thing before! We're Karen and believe the Karen Way."

How could God's message penetrate such darkened minds and hearts, we wondered. The Karen listened, but as far as we could see, they had no inclination to believe and no spiritual understanding. Yet God's Word says that "the gospel is the power of God unto salvation." Would his power reach into their minds?

As we walked from village to village on the plain, the mountains always loomed in the distance. We tried to imagine the villages hidden behind those mountain ranges and the people who had never heard about Christ, and we remembered again the promise from Isaiah, "Prisoners may be snatched, even from a strong man."

When the rainy season ended in October, we planned our first trek to the mountains. We had learned enough language to carry on a simple conversation and tell the stories from the big poster pictures. My heart beat faster as I prepared, and I could sense Jim's excitement. It wasn't even dampened when Abel and Louie, who agreed to help us carry our packs, wouldn't carry my pack because I was a woman.

We packed our sleeping bags and took some food—rice,

packets of dried soup and sweetened condensed milk—to supplement the rice and peppers meals the Karen fed us. Trekking was tiring, but it was fun to wade through the creeks as they splashed over rocks, walk along the trails, and enjoy the rugged beauty of the hills. By evening of the first day we were on a ridge about 3,000 feet above Wangloong. We couldn't reach a village that night so we camped along the way, cooked a pot of rice and a packet of soup and kept the fire going to keep the snakes and wildcats away.

By late afternoon of the second day we entered the clearing of the first village where a gnarled old man with a terribly disfigured face and matted hair came out to greet us. He was clad only in a short tunic, and he held a huge melon in one hand while he slashed it open with his field knife in his other hand. He grinned horribly as he walked slowly toward us holding out a slice of melon while juice dripped down his arms in dirty rivulets. I was too terrified to run and too scared to realize he was trying to be friendly. Later we learned that a bear had mauled and scarred his face.

In Karen culture the headman is supposed to entertain strangers, so we asked for directions to the headman's house, and he promptly invited us up onto his porch. As we talked we watched his wife clean a bucket of small frogs. With her thumb she quickly disemboweled them and dropped them into a pot of boiling water. Soon we realized she was preparing our supper, but we were so hungry and it smelled so good, we gladly dipped into the common bowl when the food was ready.

At meal time the Karen sit on the floor around a tray of food, and each person uses the "family" spoon. The bowl of frog stew, hot and peppery, sat on the tray with steaming rice piled around it. Karen eat rice with their fingers, and they're so skillful not a grain sticks to their hands. But this was my first try, and I soon had gummy rice all over me. Feeling sorry for this clumsy foreigner, the lady of the house kindly set an old chipped enamel spoon in front of me.

That evening we played the gospel records and soon drew a crowd onto the headman's porch. Using the posters and simple words, Jim explained that God created all things. He loved the Karen people, but the Karen people forgot God and began to worship the spirits. Satan is the head of the spirits. But God still loves the Karen people and wants them to return to Him. He sent His Son, Jesus, into the world in form of a man, and He did many marvelous things like healing sick people. He was good, but bad people hated Him, and they put Him to death on a cross. Jesus took the punishment for our sins on the cross and died for us so that we can be forgiven and have eternal life in heaven. After three days Jesus rose from the dead. He had defeated Satan and the spirits. He is stronger than Satan, and if you believe in Him, He will deliver you from the spirits.

We hoped they understood at least some of the faltering words, but instead of asking more about the message, they wanted to know, "How much did you pay for your shirt?" "Do you have medicine for my sick child?" "Do foreigners eat rice?"

Our hearts sank. Tired and disappointed, we rolled out the sleeping bags, and the headman's wife came over to inspect these funny "blankets." The Karen have only a thin cotton blanket and as we each crawled into our own bag we heard someone remark, "No wonder they don't have children."

For ten days we trekked from village to village. The Karen are very hospitable, so we tried to arrive in time for supper. But our white faces frightened some. At one village we bought a chicken, hoping they would fix us a meal, but they ate the chicken themselves and served us only peppers.

Climbing through the tall pines between villages gave us time away from the people to reflect. What did we expect? We knew this was Satan's stronghold. Did we think he'd release his hold, and the people would come running to hear the gospel? On the mountain ridges we could see a panorama of valleys and winding creeks, the nests of villages, and patches of rice fields. What a privilege to be here, we told each other, then prayed that God would work by His power among the Karen people and release them from the grip of the Strong Man.

Back in the villages, however, were the unwashed faces, and clothes stiff with grime, the bodies covered with sores, and the minds hard or blank towards the gospel. We knew that this was Satan's territory. We sold simple medicines for sore eyes, malaria and ulcers, but our hearts ached as we saw cases that were beyond our help. Some would find temporary relief in the smoky haze of the opium pipe. Everyone old enough to hold a pipe either smoked or chewed betel nut. I watched in amazement as a nursing baby grabbed his mother's pipe and shoved it into his own tiny mouth.

One village was definitely not friendly, and we wondered if the villagers were involved in opium trade. Abel and Louie were in a bad mood because they had run out of cigarettes and had no place to buy more, so they threatened to go home early. On top of that, for nearly every meal, the Karen fed us a fermented bean paste with rice that smelled and tasted horrible. Even the carriers could hardly eat it. People didn't invite us up to their porches, and even after we had dressed a nasty wound and given them medicine, they still didn't let us sleep there. "Oh, you can go on in the moonlight," they told us.

Playing the records produced various reactions. In most places people thronged to us, pressing as closely as possible to see and hear. In one place a modern Zaccheus even climbed a tree for a better view.

"Be quiet and listen! This is the Truth," some exclaimed as they bent closely to hear every word. Some tried to sing the songs. Others remained silent or questioned us.

"Would you have us change our customs?" an elder asked.

"We want you to return to the God who created you in the beginning." Jim answered.

"But our fathers and grandfathers worshiped the spirits. It would be better to die than to change now."

"Is it really true that we can get rid of the spirits?" queried another man.

"Yes, Jesus Christ can deliver you from the spirits."

"I'm going to turn, then," he said promptly.

"If you do, I will, too," another chimed in.

"Who else has believed?" he wanted to know. When he found out no one had believed yet, he decided to wait a while and walked away.

Rumors circulated quickly: a big giant in America eats Karen children. The foreigners kidnap children. A few had heard that some Sgaw Karen had believed and they all died. Others told us that the headman said they shouldn't let the foreigner into their house. Some said we ate human flesh because they saw containers in our house with the Quaker Oats man or the Gerber baby on the outside. Some thought hot dogs were human fingers and catsup was human blood. The devil magnified all these lies in order to scare people away from us.

We realized quickly that we couldn't convince them or even make them understand. Only God could shine into their dark minds and reveal the Truth to them by His Spirit. That season we made six trips, spending 46 days on the trail and reaching 47 villages.

Back in Wangloong our field leader visited us. "What shall we do?" we asked. "No one is interested." He suggested that we set some prayer goals for the coming year and see what God would do. So we decided that during the next year we'd ask God for two requests: some way to live in a Karen village, and that the first Karen would come to Christ.

Long months passed before God began to answer. Jim was away when a Karen came from nearby Sandy Creek and asked me to come to see a boy who had slashed his leg with a field knife. He had a badly infected knee and they had brought him home on the back of an elephant. I dressed it, gave him medicine, and went back every day to change the dressing.

Another man from Sandy Creek came. "Can you help my wife?"

"What's wrong with her?" I asked.

"She gave birth to twins and doesn't have enough breast milk to feed them both." We were expecting our first child and had supplies on hand, so we showed him how to mix up powdered milk and feed it to the babies in a bottle. Such a little thing, but it meant life or death to those babies who flourished and eventually grew fat. And it opened the door to Sandy Creek Village.

Headman Spider was now old, and the new headman, Saturday, was impressed with our medicine and asked us to come live in a house right on the edge of the village. They would allow this by pulling in their invisible village fence a bit, just behind the house we would rent. We would be in for all practical purposes, but were not bound to participate in village ceremonies and taboos. God had answered our first prayer.

We set about trying to minimize the difference between our way of living and theirs, while still maintaining some efficiency and our health. Armed with mops, rags and buckets of water, we besieged the tiny wooden house. After spraying, we disposed of eight scorpions, one mouse and innumerable cockroaches. Then we tried to figure out how to furnish this house as simply as possible. We could do without curtains, except for the bedroom. Books set us apart but were essential to our work. There wasn't room for a bed, just a mattress on the floor which was just as comfortable. Local enamel dishes would be less conspicuous than our plastic melamine.

By now our first baby, Linda, had been born. She just fit into a little car bed which sat on the edge of our mattress and wa the focus of much attention.

"You don't feed her rice?" they wondered. And "why do you lay her on her tummy?" They laid their babies on their backs. They also wondered why I held her over my shoulder and burped her. And why we put her in a separate bed from ours. Their babies always sleep with them. One day I was standing in front of our house holding her in my arms when a lady came by and wanted to hold her. When she held out her arms to take her I saw her hands were crippled with leprosy. I recoiled and held my baby tightly. Even if it meant a loss of face, I couldn't give my baby to her.

The first weeks our home served as a preaching chapel, nursery, display house and entertainment center. Records played perpetually and Jim had plenty of opportunities to explain the gospel posters on our wall. Children baby-sitting their little brother or sister toted them to our house to be amused. Our belongings and way of living and eating were all duly inspected. No matter how simply we lived, they always told us, "You have so much stuff!"

We were always on call for playing records, selling medicines, taking photos and spraying houses (the spray was so effective in our home). Few were genuinely interested in the gospel, but we were gaining proficiency in the language and we felt we were gaining deeper insight into how they lived.

One day we invited a Karen single lady to eat lunch with us. Because she had never married she was despised. She wore the long white dress of single ladies, but it was filthy. Her hands looked like they had never been washed. Dirt caked under her long stained fingernails. Inside the house she saw my bread dough rising in a bowl. Plunging her fingers into the puffy dough she asked, "What's this?" I looked at the deep dirty imprint and was glad we'd be baking the bread so her germs would die before we ate it. She gobbled the rice and stew we served, then without thanking us, she walked into our back yard and stripped off the ripe eggplants growing in our garden. Maybe she felt if we invited her to eat she could also help herself to anything she wanted. Was this what Jesus meant when He told us to invite those who cannot repay us, and we will be repaid by Him?

Abel and Louie, who once seemed interested and had heard the gospel many times now seemed distant and cold. Headman Monday asked, "You've been living in Sandy Creek. What does that headman say about your Jesus? Is he going to turn? If he turns, then I can, too, but if he doesn't, I can't." How was God going to answer our prayer for the first believers? Our field leader wrote a letter trying to encourage us. "You must wait for God's time." But the year was soon coming to an end.

We were surprised one day when some Thai Christians came to our door. "We live five miles down the river," they told us, "and our teacher from the city can't come for our Christmas service. Could you come instead?" We didn't even know there was a small Thai leprosy church there, but Jim agreed to go.

Most of the patients were Thai, but a Karen family who had been put out of their own village had sought refuge there, including Mrs. Glass who had been cast out of her village because people accused her of having an evil spirit. The Thai Christians had given her a warm welcome. "We are not afraid of spirits," they told her. "We believe in Jesus. He is stronger than the spirits."

On Christmas Day Jim met the three Karen people. They had been touched by the love shown them, but they couldn't understand the Thai language, so they really had not understood the gospel. They were overjoyed when Jim explained it to them in their own language, and they were ready on the spot to renounce the spirits and accept Christ.

After the Christmas service and feast, Jim returned to tell us that God had answered our second prayer goal: for the first

Pwo Karen in our area to believe in Christ. Mrs. Glass and Mr. and Mrs. Silver became the first Pwo Karen believers. We couldn't have had a better Christmas present.

# 5

## GREAT DISAPPOINTMENT
### 1961-1969

We began the year 1961 aware that God had answered our two prayer goals—we were living in a Karen village, and several Karen had turned to Christ. What a great start for the work. Soon, we thought, we'd have a thriving church.

One of the new believers, Mrs. Glass, was the daughter of Headman Lite, in Crabs Pond, a very large village on the plains, so Jim made several trips to the village with Mrs. Glass, hoping that her joy in the Lord would stir her friends and relatives. Instead, they told her, "when we're cast out of the village we might turn to Jesus, too." Marginal people like Mrs. Glass and Uncle Silver, we learned, did not have much influence on so-called normal people.

Then Shway Po came to help us and Boy Jee and his family turned. They were the first "normal" Karen family living in a Karen village to come to Christ. Soon after that came Mr. and Mrs. Gawk and Mrs. Pot. God was building his church.

After that first baptism Jim came in beaming. "What a great time! Six long years, but we finally saw Karen actually make a public stand for Christ in front of their friends. We wondered what our church friends back home would think of being baptized in a flooded rice field? How different it was from the velvet draped baptistery in most of our churches. Would they understand the significance of this major step in the life of a tribal person?

We held the first Karen Believers Conference at the time of the baptism, and Karen Christians met together for their very first communion service. We served cold cooked rice instead of wafers, and passed a common cup of red Kool Aid. The Karen had no Bible or hymnbook in their own language, but they listened intently as Jim explained a Bible story using the flannel graph figures. How strange those Bible characters looked in long hot robes, and long hair and beards. They didn't look like either themselves or the foreigner, yet the story held their interest. Now was the time to pour into them as many Bible stories as their minds could absorb. The Karen thought that God was like the big Buddha idols they saw in the Thai temples nearby. To change that mindset we told Bible stories, and they began to get a new idea of God as the Creator, as a God who is just and holy, as a Father who loves them and cares for them, as a Savior who was willing to die for them, as a living person who heard and answered their prayers.

Now we had to help them grow. Jim had translated some portions of Scripture, so he began to teach Boy Jee to read his own language. Boy Jee tried, valiantly tried, but it just didn't click for him. His wife and kids, peering at the lessons over his shoulder, caught on, but he struggled in vain. No matter how many hours he poured over those pages, repeating the words after Jim, it didn't make sense.

About that time some great changes took place in the area. The new Yanhee Dam formed a lake which covered most of the Thai leprosy village where Mrs. Glass and Uncle Silver lived. It covered most of Wangloong market, Sandy Creek where Boy Jee, Mr. and Mrs. Gawk and Mrs. Pot lived, and it covered many other villages Karen villages as well. The government offices and the Wangloong market moved up the road to the

Hod-Maesariang crossroads. A few Karen chose to stay on high ground, but Mrs. Glass with Uncle Silver's family moved to another rehabilitation village. The once-bustling area around Wangloong turned into a ghost town. Finally we moved up to Mae Tang, along with Gawks, Boy Jees, Abel, Headman Saturday and other Karen families.

In the enthusiasm of their new faith, the Christians began to collect materials for a simple church building. They cleared a site, cut poles and bamboo for siding, and prepared roofing. Then, slowly, like a dream crumbling, the tiny group of new believers began to fall apart. Mr. Gawk lost interest in attending services and wouldn't help Boy Jee put up the building. In fact the Gawks and the Boy Jee family seemed to compete with each other over which one could get the most out of the missionary.

Knowing how much the Karen loved to sing, Jim spent hours translating hymns into Pwo Karen. And because they couldn't read the Scriptures, he packed these songs full of doctrine. They didn't have any problem memorizing the words as we taught them. Boy Jee's oldest daughter, Date Mung, had a lovely, clear strong voice. She knew all the songs and sang them beautifully. But then she chose not to be baptized with her parents, thinking it would jeopardize her chances of a good marriage. When a popular young man asked to marry her, her parents objected.

"But he's not a Christian," they told her.

"If you don't let me marry him, I'll hang myself," she threatened. Suicide was a common occurrence among young people, and couldn't be taken lightly.

The boy talked about becoming a Christian, but his well-to-do parents said they'd cut off his share in the inheritance if he did. Then after the wedding, he became badly addicted to opium. Date Mung's promising future had burst like a bubble.

Next the Boy Jee family had a new baby whose eyes became infected and wouldn't respond to medication. When she developed a hydroencephalic condition, non-believers called her "the Jesus baby" and urged her parents to try spirit practices to cure it. "Jesus hasn't helped," they jeered. "The foreigner hasn't helped. Medicines and doctors haven't helped. This is what you get for forsaking the demons and worshiping Jesus." The Boy Jee family couldn't even turn to God's Word or fellow Christians to strengthen them in the face of such taunts.

Mrs. Pot's husband, now out of jail, was impressed to see how she had prospered. He had broken with opium in jail and now wanted to become a Christian. He was baptized and seemed to have a very keen mind to learn. Soon, however, his friends tempted him and he went back to opium; then he stole to support his habit. Mrs. Pot and her children again showed signs of starvation as her husband sucked every penny into his opium pipe.

One day in church Mr. Pot got angry because Jim refused to marry a Christian girl to a non-Christian man. He picked up a wooden plank and came after Jim with threats. Jim grabbed the board and surprised Mr. Pot with his strength, and Mr. Pot backed away, realizing he had picked on someone stronger than he was.

We thought it was hard work to get the first believers to turn. Now we realized it's even harder to make disciples out of new believers. The death-threatening crisis of believing was exciting compared to the daily grind of obedience. New habits of regular attendance at meetings clashed with opportunities to work and earn money on Sundays. Prayer to an unseen God seemed so nebulous compared to the intricate way of demon worship with tangible sacrifices.

Mrs. Gawk developed severe chronic headaches that didn't respond to medication and asked, "If I'm a Christian, why doesn't God heal me?" She began to doubt God's goodness and power and was tempted to worship the spirits again. With that Mr. Gawk decided the Jesus Way was too hard, so he quit coming to services, and finally exploded, "If I had known the Jesus Way was this hard, I wouldn't have become a Christian." Jim reminded him that he had had little choice—he was in a desperate condition when he believed. Finally, after piling up debts to their neighbors, the Gawks moved away.

We prayed even more for Abel and Louie, our language helpers. They were intelligent young men who could read and write both Thai and Karen. If they would turn to Christ it would give the new group of believers some dynamic leadership. At times they seemed very close, then Louie was offered another job with better pay and moved away. Old Priest Monday's wife became sick with stomach cancer. In desperation he turned to Jesus, hoping she would be healed. But she died. Bitterly disappointed that the Jesus "magic" didn't work, he turned back to demons. Abel, too, refused to turn. "Jesus might protect me if I turn, but the demons would take revenge on my relatives who don't turn," he reasoned. We had prayed for these two men more than any others. They clearly understood the Way. People at home had prayed. We sensed the Spirit of God striving with them, but to this day they have never turned to the Lord.

Jim and I wondered, "What will it take for a Karen person to believe in Jesus?" It seemed necessary for a group of Karen people to believe together. But their intricate system of social relationships was so complicated, it was virtually impossible to get a group to take the crucial step together.

Meanwhile the leaves for the church roof rotted and the other materials were sold. Boy Jee and his family moved back to Sandy Creek. We left for home assignment, and while we were away, Mr. Pot broke into our house and stole our generator. Some time later he died and Mrs. Pot married another opium addict.

Confused and puzzled, Jim and I prayed, "Lord, what about the promises?" What about the verses from Isaiah? Can prisoners from a tyrant ever escape? Will God ever save our Karen children? After ten years of pioneer work on the plains, we had seen God work in a glorious and wonderful way, and those first five baptisms looked so promising, but now it seemed that Satan had plucked back these folks who once worshiped him. Only Boy Jee and his wife remained faithful, but they seemed so weak as lone believers in a sea of unbelief.

Could Karen hearts ever change from their traditional ways to new godly ways? Could they ever prove that Jesus is stronger than the devil? Would any Karen be able to withstand the pressure from their non-believing neighbors? Would they ever see that their greatest need was to trust God whether or not they were sick or well? We seemed to be hitting our heads against a spiritual brick wall. What were we doing wrong, we asked ourselves. We had tried everything we knew to do, but after ten years, there was still no viable Pwo Karen church. We were discouraged and we were heart broken.

# PART II
# IN THE MOUNTAINS
## 1969-1979

*The church at Striped Creek*

# 6

## NEW START IN THE MOUNTAINS
### 1969

The mountains of North Thailand dominate the land-scape, and they reminded us, wherever we traveled on the plain, that most of the Pwo Karen lived there as virtual prisoners of the Strong Man. Roads now penetrated the areas we had trekked before, and on his new motorcycle Jim could get to the villages on the Omkoy ridge in a couple hours instead of a couple days. Still, we couldn't live in a Karen village until we had permission from the village headman.

Six years before this we had tried to move to the mountains. We had rented a tiny bamboo house in the Thai market of Na Fawn and visited the nearby Karen villages. Some Thai shop-keepers we knew from Wangloong had moved up to Na Fawn to sell salt, thread, dried fish and yarn to the Karen who walked in from surrounding villages. When the Karen came to town, they were shocked to see foreigners, but when we called to them in their own language, they visibly relaxed, smiled, and often stayed to listen to the gospel records, giggling and poking each other at what they heard.

Besides trucks and Land-Rovers, cattle trains on their way to Omkoy or Burma stopped just outside our front door. In the evening Jim sat and talked with the drivers. One train had 98 cows each carrying two baskets yoked together over its back. All 98 cowbells began ringing at 4:00 a.m. the next morning as the owners hitched them up for an early start.

Striped Creek was the nearest Karen village—about two miles away—then Big Striped Creek, Splashing Creek, and, farther down the ridge road, Floating Fields and Prosperity Fields, and finally, 26 miles down, was the Thai town of Omkoy. This area has the largest concentration of Pwo Karen villages in Thailand. West of Striped Creek and the Omkoy Ridge Pwo Karenland stretched out to the border of Burma, 3,000 square miles of mountain terrain with about 300 Pwo Karen villages with no Christians.

The air at 3,500 feet above sea level was invigorating, cooler than on the hot, humid plains, but our house in the market was always damp and cold, and the children were constantly sick. When our third child, Nathan, was born, we put a plastic cover over the top of his mosquito net to keep the mist from soaking his bed. Washing and drying diapers for three children was a challenge. When wet weather kept them from drying, we rigged up a bamboo, dome-shaped basket over a hibachi and draped the wet diapers over the basket. They got yellow and smoky, but at least they dried.

For a year we trekked to the villages, mingled with Karen in the market, prayed, and waited expectantly for a sign of interest in the gospel. Often I wondered why I was there. Why was I one hundred miles away from the mission home and friends and thousands of miles from my family? We had spent six years of our lives to bring the gospel to these people. Jim had traveled widely from village to village, but no one wanted to hear the Good News; no one had turned, no churches were planted.

Had God failed us? Was He like "a stream that dried up," as Jeremiah put it? Then I remembered that when Jeremiah complained, God told him to "Repent and get on with it." So that's what we did. We believed God would do His work in His own time among the Pwo Karen. Still we couldn't help but ask,

"Lord, when will that be?"

Then one night Jim got up to get one of the children a drink and found a big mess on the door of our little refrigerator. Looking up he saw a long snake in the rafters. He reached for his field knife and tried to hack it, but hit the rafter instead. With another swipe he whacked off its tail, but the snake fled. The next day it came back and our neighbor finished it off.

I felt lonely one day so I played a tape of choir music my mother had sent me. In my mind I could see the choir members in their robes in a big comfortable warm church singing, "Sweet Hour of Prayer." They hadn't the slightest idea what life was like out here at the end of nowhere, what it was like to cook cabbage for the tenth meal in a row, or wonder if your child is sick enough to make the 100-mile trip to see the doctor. I turned the tape off and hurled it across the room.

Was God good? Of course, I knew that. I believed it. But when I could see only the mold, the mud and the dirt, the runny noses, the dusty roads, the distrustful people with their unreasonable demands, I could only believe it by faith. After living in Na Fawn for a year with no opening into a Karen village, we moved back down to the plains.

Now five years later we were going to try again with a new strategy. The Hudspiths decided to concentrate on Prosperity Fields, a big village on the new road to Omkoy where old Headman Waters lived. They bought a little house in the center of the village where they camped out two weeks at a time.

We decided to make regular visits to Striped Creek Village, the big gateway Karen village on the Omkoy ridge we could drive to. True friendship with these folks, we believed, would surely build bridges to their hearts.

One day when white puffy clouds scuttled across a Kodachrome blue sky we packed supplies on the motorcycle and began to climb. High on the mountain we could see Thai and Lawa villages, as well as clusters of Karen villages nestled in the hills. Patches of green hill rice fields clung to steep plunging hillsides, while narrow strips of bright green paddy fields hugged the bottom of the valleys. Far off in the haze beyond the next mountain range we could see the Ping River winding down the Wangloong valley.

As we rode into Striped Creek, children ran and hid their faces in their mother's skirts. Women paused in their weaving, and the rice pounder creaked to a halt as people stopped and stared at us. We crawled up the ladder of the house of Headman Note, a little man who wore a western shirt and had a western haircut. He was squatting on his porch whittling out a new axe handle. His wife sat near him feeding one of her many children. Her brilliant red tunic lavishly embroidered in green, blue, and yellow yarn, and her intricately woven red striped skirt, told us she was both a skillful weaver and an important lady. Pounds of black, white, blue, red and yellow beads hung around her neck. Her mouth was stained dark red from chewing betel nut. When we greeted them in Karen language, grins spread over their broad faces. "Where did you come from?" "Did you bring medicine?" "Are you going to stay overnight?" Mrs. Note, bold and brassy, begged "Give me your shirt. My life is so hard—I have to cook rice and feed all the visitors, and we don't even have enough rice to feed ourselves."

When we walked through the village, we found most folks friendly but cautious. A young wife smoking her pipe asked for medicine to cure the skin disease that disfigured her face. A father inquired about medicine for his wheezing child, but his wife protested "No, don't take it! It's not good!" A young couple invited us to sit down in their tiny shelter. "When are you going to come live here? Tell us, is worshiping Jesus better than worshiping the demons? Our little child died last year. The demons have not been good to us."

We passed some ladies squatting beside a bonfire on the ground outside their house. "When are you coming to live here?" they called.

"As soon as you help us build a house," I replied. And when I come I'll put on a Karen skirt."

"Yes, and you must put on a Karen blouse and beads, too, and tie a cloth around your hair. Then you will really be like us Karen."

"And when I come you must teach me to speak your language."

"Oh, we will! And you can teach us your language, too."

"No," another one protested. "The English language is too hard. Didn't you hear Uncle trying to speak some of their words? All he could make was funny ssh-ssh sounds."

The conversation went on. "What I really want to teach you is books. Would you like to learn to read?"

"Oh, we could never learn books. You can teach the children, but we women are too old to learn books."

"But you learned how to weave," I insisted. "If you studied a little bit each day you'd soon learn how to read. Did you know God has something very special He wants you to know? He has sent you His Book, and when you learn to read you can read it for yourself and find out what God wants to say to you."

Encouraged by the openness, we hurried back to Headman Note's house and broached the idea. "Build a house here?" He wouldn't hear of it. "No, that would not be good. Your beliefs are too different from ours. But, well, maybe a shack for short visits. That wouldn't be a proper house. Of course, I'll have to ask the village demon priest."

His wife laughed loudly and spat a shot of red betel juice between the porch boards. "How much will you pay us?"

Disappointed, we climbed on the motorcycle and headed back down the mountain.

The next time we visited the mountains, we found some sickness had overtaken Striped Creek. Villagers were lying on their porches, many too weak to sit up or eat. Some had been there for weeks without bathing and care, and were black with soot and dirt. The headman's aged mother crouched miserably in her hut apart from the rest of the family because of demon taboos. "Yes, the demon way is very hard," she moaned. Her patriarch husband, a wise man full of folklore, but strongly Buddhist, had been one of four leading men in the village who had recently died. People wondered what they had done that had offended the spirits and brought such disaster upon them.

We bathed some faces and offered medicine. Most of them took it. In one smoke-filled room a weary mother sat beside the wasted form of a teenage girl, giving her sips of warm water, adjusting her blanket, easing her position.

"We sacrificed two pigs to the demons yesterday," the father told us. We noticed that her wrists were tied with new string. A Thai quack had given her three injections and had charged them an outrageous price, but nothing had helped. We prayed that she would take our medicine, but her parents refused. The girl died the next day, but others who had taken our medicine lived.

That was all the push that Headman Note needed. He was so impressed he not only gave us permission to build, he chose the spot for us himself, near the edge of the village. Karen men helped us build a house, making it as much like theirs as possible with a big front porch and a fire box on the front room floor. Karen men cut posts and sawed boards out of pine trees. When the materials were ready they called the village men together and put it up all in one day. Once again God had answered prayer and used medical help to open the door for us to live in a village. And now Jim, whom the Karen called Jo Dee, had the chance to build friendships with the men.

Our youngest child, Nathan, and I arrived on a big rice truck with all our belongings. It had begun to rain, and the truck driver pulled up about a half-mile from the village and told us to get out.

"But we're not there yet," I protested. "How do we get our stuff the rest of the way?"

"Well, I can't go any further," he insisted. "I might get stuck."

Then, seemingly out of nowhere, a Karen man appeared and convinced the driver to go the rest of the way. Later, I wanted to thank the man, but couldn't find him, and I wondered if God had sent an angel to watch over us.

One day soon after we moved into the village Jim came home very excited. Geekay, a neighbor, had agreed to take Jim through a one-year cycle showing him what Karen do in preparing fields, planting rice, weeding, harvesting, making fences. He would also teach us what kind of demon ceremony is required at each phase. We wouldn't have to participate in the ceremonies, but we could watch and learn.

Planting rice side by side with them and squishing our feet in the mud was fun, but our backs ached from bending over and pressing each plant into a muddy row. Harvesting was more fun, beating the dried sheaves against the mat until all the golden grains had fallen off the stalk. It was good for them to see that we were human, that we got tired and hungry and made mistakes. One Karen leaned over close to Jim, peered in his face and asked, "Jo Dee, can you really see with those blue eyes?"

All day long the Karen watched what we did, how we did it, what we ate. It was like being on TV for 18 hours a day. They sat by our fire or stood by our kitchen door watching.

"Why do you boil all that water?" they asked. "We can drink it without bothering to boil it."

"And look at all those dishes they wash! We only have a tray and one bowl."

One old man used to watch for a while then turn away shaking his head, "Tsk! Tsk! Those foreigners! They're always cleaning their things."

I often wonder how we managed up on the mountain, 30miles from a fresh market and 90 miles from Chiangmai where we could buy flour and dry milk? We brought in about a month's supply of staples, but we never knew how many mouths we'd have to feed. Visitors couldn't phone to say they were coming. Sometimes they brought food, though, and sometimes Karen shared beans or melons they grew or mushrooms or bamboo shoots they had gathered in the jungle.

Sometimes our garden yielded produce. One way or the other God always provided for us.

Once we were nearly out of supplies when a group of about 20 Karen from a faraway village arrived. For a moment I panicked. How would I feed them? Then I remembered a jar of dry soy beans that had been sitting on our shelf for months. The Karen don't usually eat soy beans, but when I fixed them into a stew with tomato paste and peppers to eat with rice, they liked it and it was nourishing for them. God supplied abundantly—better than if we had sat down and planned out each day's menu.

Karen people eat the poorest diet of any tribal people I know—rice and hot chili peppers three times a day. Most children are malnourished. They rarely eat fruit or vegetables, and they eat meat only when they make a sacrifice. Bananas are nourishing and easy to grow, so we tried to encourage them to plant more banana trees, but the spirits allowed them to plant bananas only in a few select places. Other places were taboo. We gave them seeds to plant tomatoes and papaya, but they said, "Oh, you plant them and we'll eat them."

Karen custom demands that they share their food. If I have beans, I'll give you some today; then tomorrow you must give me some of your beans. But if they plant something different like peas—which no one else grows—they must give it all away and can't collect back in kind. Such bondage killed any incentive to progress.

We were asked to help a little child who was nearly blind with vitamin A deficiency. "Don't you have a garden?" we asked, knowing that pumpkins and papaya would prevent such deficiency.

"Oh, yes, we have a garden." They showed us a well fertilized spot, but it only had big beautiful tobacco plants in it—not healthful food.

Meanwhile we were learning more of the Karen ways. One time Geekay took Jim to his former house site. He dragged a stick along the way calling the spirits to follow. When he got to the place where his ladder used to be, he pulled a long white rooster feather out of his bag. "Come back, come back! I'm feasting you with a big white chicken."

"But you don't have a chicken—you just have a feather," Jim protested.

"Oh, Jo Dee, we can't give a chicken every time! We fool them sometimes, and they fool us sometimes!" Geekay grinned sheepishly.

Our children loved our simple home in the village and often opened opportunities for us to talk to people. The slide pictures on their View Master especially caught the fancy of the Karen. One morning we were awakened at four in the morning by a crowd buzzing outside our window. They wanted us to get up so they could see the "movies."

Karen children showed our kids how to carve a wheel out of a board to make a wheelbarrow, how to shoot with a slingshot, and to enjoy eating flying ants. Nathan soon spoke the language better than we did.

Their most felt need, though, was for medicine. We thought this would be the bridge that would bring us close to them. At first, even though they saw that people who ate the medicine got well, they were still reluctant to take it. Perhaps the village elders told them the demons would be angry if they ate the white man's medicine. Sometimes they tried the spirit way first—making a sacrifice or tying their wrists. If that didn't work they came for medicine from us. When we gave it to them, we made it a point to pray aloud to God for healing and told them not to do demon worship. We couldn't prevent them from doing demon worship behind our backs, but we wanted them to know that healing comes from God.

They came in a steady parade, shaking with malaria, burning with fever, carrying emaciated babies. They came with burns, badly infected cuts and all kinds of worms. One day I gave a boy some worm medicine. They next morning people told me I had killed him. He had taken the medicine and had passed out. Had I given him the wrong medicine or the wrong dosage? I hurried to where he lived, an hour away, and found him sitting on his porch beaming. It was the right medicine and the right dosage and he had just passed a huge wad of worms.

We noticed a pattern emerging. God was allowing a crisis to occur in every household in the village—a crisis where we could help in a dramatic way to demonstrate that Jesus was stronger than the evil powers. He could do what no other power could do. He was showing these Karen, who had followed their fathers' and grandfathers' tradition, that He had another way for them. They didn't have to worship evil spirits. This was revolutionary thinking for them. For two years God worked in such a way that they couldn't deny His power. Anthropologists who came to study the Pwo Karen people used the same medicine we used, but it didn't work as well. While we were in the village no one died, though some died when we were away.

The spiritual battle seemed to converge at the point of sickness. Would Jesus make them well or not? If they got well, maybe they would believe, but if they didn't get well, then they might as well worship the spirits. We were not doctors; we had no guarantee that medicine would cure all sickness, but we knew that God was the Great Physician as well as Creator. He was building His church and the gates of hell could not prevent it. If He chose to reveal His power by healing people, that would bring glory to Him. If they died He could defend His own Name, and He would do it in His own time and in His own way, but we longed to see the breakthrough with our own eyes. Meanwhile we searched for other bridges to get through to them.

Karen love to sing, so we made a big chorus book and began to teach the young people to sing choruses about Jesus. They liked the catchy tunes, but suddenly no one came any more. The village elders had warned them, "If you learn the Jesus songs you will forget Karen ways."

Disappointed, we built another bridge. A health organization gave us a supply of powdered milk which we mixed and served to the children who were so poorly nourished. They loved it, but in a short time they refused to drink it. Then we learned they had been forbidden to drink "that ogre's milk" lest "the foreigner kidnap you and take you to the ogre in America that eats Karen children." They firmly believed that preposterous lie! Another bridge had closed.

Next we tried to teach them to read books in their own language. The teenagers wanted desperately to learn how to read like the Thai, so we made reading primers. One boy, Jo Blay, carried firewood to earn money to buy his own book. They were making fine progress until suddenly they stopped coming. Jo Blay brought his book back and told us, "We can't read."

"Why? What's wrong?" we asked.

"The village elders told us that those who learn to read will be food for the white ogre. They say that if we learn to read we will become Christians."

Not willing to let this bridge close, Jim went to see the headman. "The government in Bangkok wants you tribal people to learn to read. We have letters that give us permission to make books for you. If you know books, then the Thai can't cheat you so much," Jim argued.

With that the headman sent his 10-year-old son, Dee Keng, to study at our house. Every morning the boy swaggered into our front room in his new white shirt and freshly combed hair. He didn't know a word of Thai, but his father insisted that he learn Thai books, not Karen. Being a bright boy he worked hard, and eventually learned to read both Thai and Karen.

One project did take hold and lasted more than twenty years. The headman's wife usually gave birth to a baby every year, but more than half of them had died. Sometimes she didn't even get home in time to deliver, and the baby was born along the trail.

I arranged to bring a Christian doctor to the village, and he brought films to show the people how planning a family can give a better life to the child and keep the mother more healthy.

Ten Karen women decided to try it. We gave them a choice of three months of birth control pills or an injection that lasted three months. They had never used a calendar, so we told them, "When the moon dies three times, come to our house," and they came faithfully. Soon we had about 250 women from different villages signed up. A few went to the hospital for a tubal ligation. Infant mortality was greatly reduced, babies were cherished and nourished, mothers felt like they were worthwhile people, and many from distant villages heard the gospel records when they came in.

In spite of all these bridges and the display of God's power, we were keenly aware that nothing was working. Medicine, milk, education, family planning—they liked the ways that we brought, but they refused to accept the Message.

Perhaps meeting other Karen Christians in action would impress them, we thought. During this time we kept in touch with the Boy Jee family down on the plain, and Mrs. Glass and Uncle Silver and their families in the new rehabilitation settlement in Gong Loy. So one weekend we gathered them together in Striped Creek for a retreat, and our neighbors heard them singing Karen hymns and praying. At night around the fire, the Striped Creek Karen listened to the Christians talking about God, and long after we went to bed we heard them pelting the Christian Karen with questions.

"How much do they pay you to become a Christian? You mean they don't pay you a monthly wage? What do they give you? Free blankets? Free sacks of rice? Is it true you really don't do any more demon worship? You don't tie strings around the wrists of your children? Aren't you afraid the demons will be angry? Can you still wear Karen clothes and eat rice even after you become a Christian?"

One or two seemed very interested, but a Karen cannot make an independent decision. He must wait for a consensus—a block of people related by blood, or a nuclear family who agree. If only one person decides for himself, he is ostracized by the others.

One day the assistant headman's wife came and sat on our porch as she often did, watching and asking questions. In a moment of frustration, I blurted out, "Why do you think we come here to tell you about Jesus? We leave our nice homes and our beloved families to come here to tell you about Jesus, but all you want is medicine!"

"Yes, that's exactly right!" she said, shaking her head. "At last you see it. All we want is your medicine; we don't want your Jesus."

Her frank statement rocked me. After years of tramping up and down the mountains, of living in their village, binding up their wounds, building bridges of friendship, praying and patiently waiting for God to open their hard hearts, I did see it—very clearly. Surely, I thought, God sees it, too. He knows. And surely they had seen God demonstrate His power among them in such dramatic ways—far beyond our human ability. When would they take that important step of faith from demons to Christ? When would they believe that He had power to break the bonds of the Tyrant and set them free?

# 7

## JESUS IS STRONGER
### 1969-1971

We hadn't slept well that night. The villagers of Striped Creek had celebrated their annual feast for the demons the night before, and each household, except ours, of course, had brought a chicken as an offering to the demon priest. Then all the men had gone to the spirit house just outside the village where they had performed a special ceremony. Feasting and drinking followed well into the night.

The next morning we were sitting down to our usual fruit and toast breakfast when a voice outside our window called, "Are you home?"

Jim got up to see who it was. "Bouy Dee fainted last night and is still unconscious," the caller said. "We think she might be dying. Please come see."

"Oh, she probably drank too much whiskey last night," Jim argued.

"No," the caller insisted, "something is really wrong. Please come!"

So we left breakfast on the table, grabbed the medicine bag, and hurried over to the new settlement just across the road. At the foot of the ladder that went up to the porch, we pointed in alarm to a pool of fresh blood and asked about it.

"Oh, we had to kill the dog," our guide explained. "It barked at the wrong time and that broke a taboo. That's probably what's causing the sickness."

We climbed a rickety ladder, bent low to enter the tiny bamboo house, and found what looked like the entire village crowded into the small room. As our eyes grew accustomed to the darkness we saw a young mother lying on the floor by the fire with a wet blanket over her. Kneeling beside her I realized she was in a coma with eclamptic convulsions. As we watched, her stomach tightened in a hard contraction, then relaxed.

No one dared to touch her, but we noticed the big bulge of her stomach had gone down. Sure enough, the baby had been born. We reached under her skirt and pulled it out. We tried to get the baby breathing, but it had turned blue. When it didn't respond, most of the villagers fled, weeping and wailing.

"It's the demons," the demon priest divined. "They've caused her sickness."

But the headman wanted our opinion. "What do you think, Jo Dee?" he asked.

"She's a very sick lady," Jim told him. "We can't treat her here. She needs to go to the hospital in Chiangmai."

Alarm showed on their faces. No Karen from this village had ever gone to the hospital and come back alive. The village men huddled in a tight circle to talk it over. Then the headman announced, "We'll do three days of big demon worship and then we will let her go."

"But if you wait, she'll die," Jim protested.

The headman considered, "I hear the demons go with the sick person right up to the hospital gate, hop off and wait on the gate post until they return, then hop back on."

After talking awhile they finally decided to let her go but send six men along to deal with the evil spirits if she died along the way. So they carried the unconscious woman out to the road and loaded her into our jeep.

Bouncing over 90 miles of rough and muddy road to Chiangmai made her convulsions more frequent, but she was still alive upon arrival. In the hospital nurses cut off all her strings and beads, tied a clean white gown on her and put her in a ward bed.

Jim came back to the village to get me to come stay with her. When she regained consciousness, she must have thought she had died and reincarnated in the next world. She had never been to the city and had never seen a room with white walls. She didn't understand a word of Thai and her beads and tribal clothes were gone. And what was this tube sticking in her arm? She tried to jerk it out, but I held it in.

"Bouy Dee, this is a hospital in Chiangmai city," I tried to explain. "You are very sick. Your baby has been born, but it did not live. We brought you up here to get well. Then we'll take you back home." She looked wildly at me, then as I spoke her language, she realized who I was and relaxed a little.

Being in the hospital was a different world to her. She had never used a toilet or slept in a bed that was up off the floor. She didn't even know how to get a drink of water from a faucet. I explained that she must eat the food, even if it wasn't peppery hot, and even if it was taboo in Karen custom for sick people to eat food. I insisted that she take the medicine, even if she had to chew the capsules before she swallowed them. And I prayed with her, telling her that medicine is a gift from God. He is the One on whom we depend. He hears and answers our prayers. He heals our sicknesses, and this is a better alternative than doing demon worship.

After ten days the hospital released her, and we brought her back to the village. In great amazement the villagers looked at her, then at us. "She was dead and you brought her back alive!" No one doubted that this was a miracle, and we thought surely they would recognize God's power in this case. It had to make some difference to them!

It did make a difference, but not the way we expected or hoped. About a month later Buoy Dee and her husband came down the road carrying bulging shoulder bags and sleeping mats. "You have been so good to us," they announced, "we're coming to live with you!" Karen love to latch on to someone whom they perceive has power. Only with great difficulty did we convince them that she would be okay in her own home.

We treated Bouy Dee many times after that. When she still complained of discomfort, we took her up to the hospital for a checkup. Another time we treated her eyes when they were swollen from conjunctivitis. Still, all she wanted from us was medicine. We talked about God's power to heal bodies and hearts, but it fell on deaf ears. Other Karen convinced her not to let us pray for her.

What would it take, we wondered, to get through to these darkened hearts? Each time someone came for help we prayed, not just for their healing, but that God would open their minds to understand His power and their need of His grace.

One day a mother brought us a listless baby that wouldn't nurse and wouldn't respond. She had gone to work in the fields and left the infant with her five-year old. Before leaving, she chewed up green banana and rice in her betel-stained mouth and left the pink sticky mass in a small, dirty blue and white whiskey cup. "If the baby cries, feed it some rice," she instructed the child.

For two days I thought the child would surely die, but every time I went to see it, it was still hanging on to life. Could Jesus help even when food and environment were so dirty? Could He reach down and touch even this tiny flickering life who was so neglected? The child swallowed a bit of medicine from a medicine dropper. Every hour I returned to force a few more drops into that tiny mouth. On the third day it was able to suck its mother's breast again.

When I filled a basin with warm water and gave the baby a bath using soap, the mother was more horrified than grateful. For a short time the baby was clean and had a chance to live, but soon it was dirty again as the mother resumed her old deeply ingrained habits. The Strong Man was not going to let go easily.

God displayed His power to Lohng Gahng as well. With

great effort this young woman walked the five miles from Splashing Creek to Striped Creek. Her tunic was so tightly stretched over her swollen stomach that she could hardly breathe or eat. Her arms and legs were skeleton thin, but a sweet smile and pleading brown eyes shone out of her emaciated face.

We took her to Chiangmai hospital where they told us she had a malignant ovarian tumor. She was in such poor condition they were afraid she couldn't sustain immediate surgery, so they kept her in for a few weeks to build up her strength for an operation. We left her there, not knowing any Thai language and without any friends.

God's timing is so beautiful! Three weeks later we returned just as they rolled her out of the operating room. She was beginning to regain consciousness, so I touched her hands and spoke gently in Karen, "It's over now; you're all done with the operation. You're okay." Her eyes fluttered open in recognition. She smiled and clung to my hands, clasping them to her breast. The next day they painted a huge purple square on her abdomen, and kept her a few weeks longer for radiation therapy. Then on Christmas Day they let us take her home, and she never had any reoccurrence of the malignancy.

A few months later she came to see me. With great care she reached into her bag and slowly unwrapped a Karen blouse which must have taken her a month to weave by hand. "You helped me very much." Her eyes shone with gratitude.

"God helped you," I answered. "He is the One who heals."

But the message just rolled off her, and we asked ourselves again "What is it going to take? What demonstration of God's power would convince them?" Yes, the Strong Man's grip was fierce, but God promised that Christ destroyed Satan's power on the cross. Satan is a defeated foe, but when would we see that victory among the Karen people?

Time and time again we saw God heal men and women in desperate conditions. Chite Kwae had cut his leg with a field knife. When his wife called us to come see him, his leg was swollen to twice the size of the good one. He had tried demon worship and sought witch doctors to blow on it, but it grew worse until now it looked like an inflated balloon that would burst any minute. We took him to the Christian clinic in Maesariang where the doctor lanced it.

While recuperating at the Maesariang clinic, Chite met Sgaw Karen Christians. He listened to the gospel records in his own language, and when we returned to take him home he was recovering nicely.

Back in the village, I went over each day to give him a shot of penicillin. Each day we reminded him that the demons had not helped him, but Jesus had surely given him life and strength.

One day he told us, "I'll make you a deal. You've been so good to me, and this medicine has helped me get well. I'm just about convinced that I'll become a Christian. If you promise to give me a sack of rice every month, then I will believe!"

I wanted to cry! How could he have missed the message so completely? Instead I stuffed back my disappointment and tried to explain, "You owe your very life to Christ. You should be grateful to him. But our giving you a sack of rice is not the way to become a Christian. You have to give up demons and decide to follow God's Way. You have to continue to make fields. It is God, not demons, who causes the rice to grow. Trust in Jesus. He'll help you." But that Way was too hard for him.

Eventually we could see that in nearly every family, God had allowed a crisis to arise that demonstrated His power to help them and opened an opportunity for us to help in a dramatic way, beyond our natural ability. The word quickly spread to villages all around.

A man who lived in a village several hours walk away was mauled by a bear that he tried to chase out of his garden. His young son appeared at our door asking for five cents worth of medicine. "What do you want it for?" I asked.

"For my dad. A bear bit him."

That was certainly unusual, but five cents worth of medicine was not going to touch it! So the son led us to his father who had been carried to our neighbor's house. Inside the dark room a 60-year-old man sat in the middle of the bamboo floor. His face was so caked with dirt and blood, we couldn't tell if his eye was torn out of its socket or not. Slowly the son lifted a piece of pink plastic covering his head and revealed a stocking cap matted with dried blood that covered the wounds on the man's head. The powerful stench nauseated us.

"Do you think we can do something?" I asked Jim.

"No, this is really bad," Jim turned away. "We'll have to take him to the hospital."

Later we heard his story. This man had gone to his garden to see how his corn was doing and noticed bear footprints.

"We have to get that bear," he told his son.

The next day when he and his son returned to the garden with a homemade gun, there was a black mother bear with two cubs. They shot the bear in the back. She whirled around and charged towards them. The father anticipated this and intended to shoot the bear in the mouth, but his gun broke just as she was nearly on top of him. He fell to his knees covering his face with his hands. When the bear started gnawing his head he cried out, "Bear, Bear, why do you bite me?" Startled at the sound of his voice she left him and ran off into the woods with her cubs.

The father's head bled profusely. Tenderly the son picked him up in his arms and took him home. For five days they tried to stop the bleeding. Finally a demon priest advised them. "It's because the rooster crowed at the wrong time of day. That is taboo. You must kill the rooster and make a sacrifice." They made the sacrifice, and the bleeding stopped, but the old man was still far from well.

Eight days after the accident, they wrapped him in a red cotton blanket and brought him to us, and we took him to the Chiangmai hospital. Later the doctor told us the bear's tooth had penetrated his skull and it was a miracle that he didn't develop meningitis.

When we saw the father all cleaned up after his operation we hardly recognized him. While he recovered in the hospital he listened to the gospel records. They were the only words he could understand because everyone else in the hospital spoke Thai.

"Uncle," we told him, "God must love you very much to spare your life. You know that bear could easily have finished you off, or you could have bled to death or you could have died from infection. The demons didn't help you, but God has helped you very much. He is stronger than the demons. He spared your life; now you are well. Why don't you turn to Him?" But he didn't want to be the only Christian in his village. The story of his remarkable recovery spread far and wide. Jesus was stronger; He could help.

In case after case God proved He was stronger than the demons. Because we helped them in these times of crises, their homes were open to us. We could crawl up the ladder to any home and be welcomed to come sit by their fire and talk. They were beginning to accept us as real people, not as strange foreigners. But no one was willing to take that crucial step to leave the demons and turn to Christ. Instead they'd take advantage of our prayer and medicine when their Karen spirits failed to heal them.

At first people in Striped Creek were impressed with God's power to heal, but gradually they rationalized that they would sacrifice to the spirits for some sicknesses, and come to the missionary for other sicknesses. In fact, now when the demon priest divined, one of his options for a "cure" was advising the person to go take the missionary's medicine. But he certainly didn't advise them to become Christians! He made it clear that "Our grandfathers and grandmothers were Karen; we will stay Karen."

Yet they knew what the gospel message was. When a team of Christians from another tribe came to give their testimonies and preach from the gospel posters, Headman Note grabbed the posters and said, "Let me explain it in our language." To

75

our astonishment he explained the gospel very clearly, but then he said, "Yes, we know. The missionary has told us all that, but we're content in our old way. We don't want to change." As a group, they had made their decision.

For twelve years we had knocked on every door we knew, expecting that a group of Karen would turn to Christ and a church would begin to function. We learned their language and customs and sought to communicate the gospel to them in meaningful terms. Many lives had been saved by medical help, and the Karen had seen God answer prayer in miraculous ways. National Christians had given their testimony of how much better it was to believe in Jesus rather than the demons. We tried to show love by helping them market their handi-crafts, and had tried to build bridges of friendship by shopping for them and giving them seeds and fertilizer to help their crops. We had transported them hundreds of miles in our jeep and spent agonizing hours preparing literacy materials and teaching them to sing and read. We had been spent long days and nights trying to help opium addicts break the habit. We had prayed and prayed for a breakthrough. People at home had faithfully prayed. But nothing had brought a single Pwo Karen soul to Christ.

About that time we met Dr. George Peters, professor of missions at Dallas Seminary, and poured out our disappointment.

"Why are you so discouraged?" he asked.

"We've been there eleven years, and we don't yet have a church planted."

"It isn't time yet," he counseled. "Normally it takes a western person going to a third culture eighteen years before a breakthrough happens. If you are an Asian going cross-cultur-ally to another Asian it will take five years. If you work with a national it will take ten years. You are right on schedule." By his analysis we still had a few more years to go.

We were stunned! Eighteen years? No one had given us a timetable. All we had was the promise that He would set the captives free. But when? And how? What Dr. Peters said seemed to fit, however, with what we were seeing.

We took some comfort from the book, *These Strange Ashes*, by Elizabeth Elliot, and were encouraged to trust God even when everything looked hopeless. From her experience we learned that faith is not when every prayer is answered immediately and everything goes well. Genuine faith is when there is a stunning array of evidence that looks as if God hasn't answered—that He has forgotten—that He isn't working. Despite outward appearances true faith believes that God is still working and that the last chapter has not yet been written.

As we drew near to another furlough we wrote to the field director. "This has been a year of retrogression instead of progress, reduction instead of multiplication, impotency instead of power, defeat instead of triumph. The Karen remain dull of understanding, darkened in mind and dead in spirit. They are covetous of material possessions, complacent in traditional ways, covert in evil deeds, and conservative in relationship to the outside world. So far the Karen have discerned no vital force in Christianity to compete with the magic of charms and ceremonies. They want the benefits gained from our living there, but reject the message we bring."

Our co-workers, Ed and Norma Lee Hudspith, decided to join another mission. Was the gospel really the power of God unto salvation that Romans 1:16 promised? Did God really have power to deliver these Karen from the demons? When we received an invitation to teach at Phayao Bible School, Jim felt we should withdraw from Karen work, first for furlough, and then to teach at the Bible School. We could still visit the Karen, and if they responded some day we could return to them.

# 8
## GOD USES WEAK THINGS
### 1969-1971

About fourteen miles down the red dirt road south of Striped Creek, fifty families had built bamboo homes there and laid out fields for peppers and rice. They called their village Prosperity Fields, and they lived under the watchful eye of wise and kind old Headman Waters. We had trekked there, slept in Headman Water's house, and told his family about Christ. One time they seemed almost on the verge of turning, but then they decided that if they became Jesus followers no one would want to marry their teenage children.

Dee Waters, the headman's son, was not so wise nor as kind as his father. He had left his first wife to marry the current Mrs. Dee who was now very sad. She had heard that her husband was sleeping with a woman on the other side of the village and she threatened to kill herself. It didn't do any good, however because young Mr. Dee continued his philandering.

One night after a hard day chopping and carrying wood, Jody, the Dee's six-year-old son, fell asleep beside the fire box. Mr. and Mrs. Dee slept on one side of the box, while the children slept on the other. Sometime during the middle of the night Jody rolled over into the hot coals and his blanket caught on fire. His screams woke up his mother, and she snatched him

*Boy Jee and his family were the first to believe in Sandy Creek*

*Married women (center) and single girls dress differently*

*Louise plays gospel recordings for the Karen children*

*Young men from the mountain area don't cut their hair*

*Gospel recordings in the Pwo language attracted many to Christ*

*Karen women weave their own clothes*

*Rich Karen use elephants for logging teak*

*Jim preaches at the Christmas celebration service in 1994*

*The Morrises' home in Striped Creek followed the Karen pattern*

*A young woman carries water on a pole*

*Eating food around a tray is a good way to fellowship*

# KAREN CHURCH LEADERS

*Bee Thout*
*Pine Village*

*Mrs. Dee*
*Prosperity Fields*

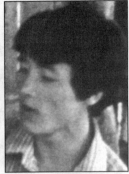

*Dee Keng*
*Striped Creek*

*Jody*
*Prosperity Fields*

*Mang Tu*
*Striped Creek*

*Jobe*
*Prosperity Fields*

*Che Louie*
*Long Village*

*Doo Boo*
*Prosperity Fields*

*Beng Vang*
*Dusty Village*

from the fire, ripped off his clothes and beat out the flames with her hands. The boy's leg and foot were badly burned, and he was in great pain.

For days and weeks Jody sat inside the house, moaning and nursing his blistered leg. Mrs. Dee had no medicine nor bandages, so she plastered the wounds with dry ashes. Gradually the pain subsided and the oozing dried up, but the top of the boy's foot had grown on to the front of his leg, so that he couldn't walk. Jody was crippled.

Mrs. Dee was devastated. "Look what you've done," she screamed. "Now, you can't walk! You'll never be able to work! How can you plow fields or plant rice? How can you harvest our crops? You'll never be able to make a living! What will we do?" A cripple in a Karen village is seen as a drag on society, and Mrs. Dee Waters loudly lamented her added burden.

After several months, Jody could scoot around, pulling himself along. But he couldn't run and haul water with the other children, and it worried Mrs. Dee until she became thin. She didn't care if her clothes were torn or dirty. She didn't bother to comb her hair. She took off her beads and bracelets, a mark of beauty to the Karen. On top of that, Mr. Dee was gone most nights, and she knew she was losing him to the other woman.

About that time Ed and Norma Lee Hudspith began visiting Prosperity Fields. For hours they squatted on the bamboo floor in Headman Water's house, explaining the gospel, but the old man just shook his head. "I've spent too many years with the spirits," he said sadly. "It's too late for me to change." Still, he allowed the Hudspiths to buy a shack next door to Mrs. Dee, so when they came to visit they'd have a place to stay.

One day Mrs. Dee stopped to talk to Norma Lee. The poor woman didn't have many friends, and not too many people smiled at her, especially not the way Norma Lee smiled. So she began spending time on the Hudspith's porch, chatting, watching Norma Lee deal with the visitors who came for medicine and listening to the small green box with the wind-up crank that told strange stories in her language.

She was especially fascinated by several large posters Ed used to tell the gospel stories. "God created the world and the first people," Ed explained. "He made a beautiful garden for the first people to live in, but they disobeyed God. They ate the fruit that He commanded they should not eat. So God had to put them out of the garden. God hasn't left Karen people, however. They have left Him, their true Maker, to follow the false way of demons."

Mrs. Dee couldn't read, and these stories weren't like the ones she had heard all her life. Which ones were right? Would the spirits become angry with her if she believed the missionary? And would Headman Waters be angry? Would it break the harmony of the village? She asked the missionary if she could have both—the spirits and this Jesus—but the missionary said, "No, you have to turn away from the spirits; you can't serve both." Something deep inside her said this was the truth.

Jody thought the foreigners looked very strange with their light hair and blue eyes, but he liked listening to the records. He squatted beside the box for hours and turned the handle until he could sing the songs and tell the stories himself.

"Jesus is greater than the spirits. He can deliver you from their power." The boy remembered when his mother had sacrificed a chicken entreating the spirits to heal his burns. "Brrrrrr, come back!" she had called them. "Come back." Then she had tied string around his wrists.

Jody was afraid of the spirits. If they were not pleased, they bit people and made them sick. Someone once told him, "Don't you know? The spirits pushed you into that fire!"

One day Ed told a story from the big black book about a man who had been lame for years. He showed a big picture of an old man lying beside a pool looking up at Jesus. Jesus told the man to get up and walk, and instantly the man jumped to his feet, completely healed, and carried his mat home.

The boy thought a lot about that story. How did he do it? Could Ed's God do that to his leg? He thought about how he'd feel if he suddenly could walk normally, and he prayed that this powerful Jesus would work a miracle in his life.

On one of their visits to Prosperity Fields, Ed and Norma Lee brought a fellow missionary, Dr. Welch, who worked in the Chiangmai hospital. He was a tall, blond Englishman who exuded a professional confidence and had a friendly smile.

Ed introduced Dr. Welch to Mrs. Dee and Jody and asked Jody if he'd let the doctor look at his leg. Jody liked the doctor immediately. Dr Welch bent over the ten-year-old boy, gently probed and studied the scarred and twisted leg, smiled at Jody to reassure him, then announced, "I believe I can fix that."

The hospital was a strange world to a ten-year old. The walls, the hospital gown, the bedding were all white, and the bed was a high, soft platform. He was afraid he'd fall off the edge in the middle of the night. The ward was filled with others in the same white gowns, but they didn't speak the Karen language. Jody couldn't even ask for a glass of water. And when they rolled him into a room with bright lights and stuck a needle into his arm, he was terrified.

"Don't be afraid, Jody," the doctor reminded him, "Jesus is your friend. He is here with you." Still, it was the scariest thing that had ever happened to him.

It wasn't a difficult operation. Dr. Welch cut the scar tissue between the ankle and the foot so that the foot could be lowered and move normally. When Jody awoke, he was back in the ward with a hard white plaster all around his leg. For a few months the new skin cracked open when he bent his leg, but gradually it healed completely with only a few burn scars on his toes. Jody could walk again. Surely this was as big a miracle as the lame man in the Bible story.

One day relatives arrived at the Dee household to announce that Old Auntie, the oldest living lady in their clan, had died. That put Mrs. Dee in line to become the demon head for all her family members related by blood. Whenever one of them became sick, they would come stay with Mrs. Dee for three days so she could perform special ceremonies and sacrifice pigs and chickens to the spirits so they'd get well.

Mrs. Dee definitely did not want to become a demon priestess. She talked long hours to the missionaries. "If I become a Christian can Jesus deliver me? Can He protect me from the demons? Could I get out of my obligations to be the demon priestess by becoming a Christian?"

"Yes," Norma Lee assured her. "Jesus is the Supreme Lord. He has greater power than the spirits. He is our heavenly Father. He loves you and wants to make you His own child."

That sounded so good to Mrs. Dee. A Father in heaven who cared. A strong Savior who could deliver her from the spirits, and from all the sacrifices and superstitions and fears that bound her. What would her husband and her father-in-law say? Would she be put out of the village, isolated, thrown out on her own?

It was a heavy decision. As Norma Lee encouraged her, she bowed her head and prayed, telling Jesus she was leaving the demon way and trusting in Him. It was a solemn moment and when she lifted her head, her face was aglow. She smiled softly as Ed took his knife and cut off the dirty blackened spirit strings from her neck and wrists. Then he cut the strings off Jody and his sister's wrists and threw them into the fire.

Jody felt a little bare, but he also felt clean. Something very significant had happened in his life. He didn't understand it all, but he was old enough and bright enough to know that this would change his life. Immediately he noticed a change in his mother, too. Norma Lee had given her a bar of soap and told her, "Take a bath, comb your hair, put on your prettiest clothes, polish your beads and bracelets and wear them. If you want your man, you have to make yourself attractive! And here's some vitamin pills to give you energy." Joy radiated from her face and she felt free from the pressure of the spirits and from her relatives. Her husband, she thought, couldn't help but notice.

One day shortly after that Mrs. Dee looked up from her rice pot to see several policeman boldly climb the ladder, stride across the room, and take down several guns hanging on the wall. Then, as she watched, they grabbed her husband, slapped handcuffs on him, hustled him into their car and drove off without telling her what was happening.

In a panic she ran to the home of Headman Waters. He explained that the store at the junction had been robbed, and bandits had held up the storekeeper at gunpoint. "Those guns," he said sadly, "were found in your house."

Soon after that the Hudspiths left for furlough and Mrs. Dee was completely on her own. When it came time to plant rice, none of her neighbors or family would help. They refused to share their plow or buffaloes. Ed left a trunk full of medicines for her to use when she got sick, but she couldn't read the directions on the labels and she couldn't remember if the malaria medicine was the white pills or the red pills, and what was the dosage. Neighbors knew she had the medicine and pestered her to share it. One thing she did remember, however: when you get sick, don't worship the demons. You pray to God.

Her new faith was soon tested. Her children became sick, but she prayed and God answered. Neighbors still refused to help her do her fields, but God gave her strength to hoe them by hand. Her family pressured her to turn back to the demons, "See, the missionary has left you all by yourself." But she knew Jesus was with her, and she refused to go back to the demon way.

Other Karen noticed how God answered her prayers even when the missionary had gone. They could not deny that God had changed Jody from a cripple to an active happy boy. Maybe Jesus could help them, too.

Occasionally on our trips to the mountains, we stopped in Prosperity Fields to encourage this lone believer and found her holding on by herself. Jody's leg was healed, but he probably would never be strong enough to do heavy field work. He was a quick learner, and needed an education, but there was no school in that village, so we arranged for Jody and his sister,

Doo Boo, to live with Mrs. Glass down on the plain. The two young people would learn to read and write in Thai, but they would also have a chance to see Thai Christians in action. So Mrs. Dee sent them off to Mrs. Glass with a big basket of rice.

# 9
## NO ESCAPING THE CALL
### 1972-1974

I slid my bare feet along the polished teak floor to make sure it was real. Our new home on the gentle green hillside overlooking shimmering Phayao Lake faced a range of purple mountains to the west. Friends often gathered on the front porch in the evenings and chatted while we watched the sun go down. I never dreamed I would live in a place this beautiful or comfortable in North Thailand.

We had returned from furlough, glad to enjoy again the fluffy rice and peppery curry, fresh pineapple and fragrant bananas. This was Thailand, with its steamy weather and tropical rains, and this was where we belonged. But we expected to be in a tribal village. To have kitchen cupboards and a stainless steel sink, electricity and appliances, even lavender gingham curtains with a matching bedspread for Linda's room, was luxury we had not had in tribal land. And, yes, a study with lots of bookshelves for Jim. I told myself, "I'm holding it all with an open hand. We didn't ask for this." But what a contrast to tribal life!

After the Pwo Karen so clearly rejected the message of Jesus, we were open to respond when our field leaders invited us to come teach at the Bible School in Phayao.

What a difference! The 48 students here truly wanted to learn God's Word. And what an opportunity to influence the whole country for Christ. One student, for example, went home on spring break and returned with this report: "Teacher, you told us to go home and win one person to Christ. I saw ten people make a decision." Another man converted at a conference, went home and won ten families to Christ. Many of these students would become leaders of the Thai church in years to come.

The Karen people, though, were always in our minds. Who would reach them? No missionary was now living among them. Once in a while one or two of them made the long bus journey to visit us in Phayao. When they saw our home they agreed this was a very nice place compared to Karenland.

From time to time we packed our sleeping bags and headed down the road to the Canaan project where Mrs. Glass and Uncle Silver stood firm in their faith. In Sandy Creek the Boy Jee family stood alone. This handful of Karen believers down on the plans were the fruit of our early years. But who would teach them? In the mountains Mrs. Dee struggled on by herself, trying to feed her children. Who would help her? And in Striped Creek where we broke our backs and our hearts for so many years? Nothing. Yet how could they hear unless someone was there to tell them? They couldn't turn on the radio and hear a gospel broadcast. They couldn't pick up a tract or book and read about God. They had no Bible nor could they read it if they had one. As far as we could tell, no one had yet responded to the message we had told them so often when we lived among them. God reinforced this promise to us from Habakkuk: I will work a work in your day, whether you believe me or not. The vision is sure. It will come to pass in my time. Be patient.

Once a year all the mission workers in North Thailand gathered for a conference. Jim and I always looked forward to this time. Colleagues working with the Hmong, the Akha and the Lisu tribes came down from the mountains. Others came from

Maehongson, where the Shan lived on the plains, or from OMF Centers at Chiangmai or Chiangrai. The conference was always a welcome balm for the bruises of daily missionary life—a time to swap stories, exchange ideas, pray and share one another's burdens. This year it was held at the school in Phayao. We cleaned dorms, scrubbed floors, raked the grounds, polishing and shining up the place for this annual event. Meetings were held in the big open chapel overlooking the lake. A rugged wooden cross hung on the wall behind the pulpit.

This year Denis Lane, one of our directors from Singapore, brought a series of messages on Abraham. "By faith," Denis reminded us, "Abraham obeyed God, leaving his country and following God to a land he didn't know." Most of us could identify with Abraham this far.

"God promised Abraham that his children would number as many as the stars in the heaven, but years passed and the promises weren't fulfilled. At one point Abraham was very discouraged." Oh, yes! Inwardly we cheered Denis on, and he continued. "So God renewed the promises and Abraham asked for a sign. Make a sacrifice,' God told him, 'And I'll accept it with fire as a sign to you that all the promises will be fulfilled.' So Abraham killed animals and laid out all the pieces of meat on the altar for the sacrifice that God required. Then he stood there waiting for God to receive the sacrifice. He waited for hours, shooing away the flies and birds, trying to keep from nodding off. Finally Abraham fell asleep, and God gave him an unsettling dream that God's people would have to go into captivity and be mistreated, but they would come back to this land. In the darkness of that night, God finally appeared as a burning flame that passed between the pieces of meat. He accepted the sacrifice with his presence, and renewed the covenant promises that Abraham's descendants and their descendants would return to this land."

The messages struck a deep chord in us. Amazing! How closely that resembled our own story. Like Abraham we had come to an unknown land. We had heard God's promises to give us spiritual children. We had laid out the sacrifices of our lives on the altar for Him, and felt like we were shooing off the flies, waiting for Him to work and fulfill those promises to build His church among the Pwo people. Yet for sixteen years nothing had happened.

In between the messages workers from each tribe reported on their work.

Doe Jones, a lean, energetic Welsh lady with blond hair pulled back in a bun, had spent over 30 years ministering to the Hmong tribal people. Leona Bair, a tall American nurse, had trekked up and down the mountains to teach the Hmong about Christ. Both these women lived in tribal houses with hewn wooden plank walls and a dirt floor. They cooked over wood fires and slept on bamboo platforms. Yet their efforts were not in vain. Numerous Hmong people had turned to Christ in many mountain villages. At least eight Hmong had learned the Thai language well enough to graduate from Bible School and were now able to teach and preach to their own people where new churches were emerging. Yes, they discussed difficult problems of how to pay national workers and how to provide church buildings, but these problems seemed far beyond the level of the Karen who had no churches or national workers.

Barb Hey and Barb Good from New Zealand also worked with the Hmong. They lived simply and poured their energies into translating the Bible and preparing a hymnbook in the Hmong language. Our Karen had no Bible or hymnbook.

Ann Burgess, with her lame leg, lived in a remote village working with a Mien church leader translating the Bible into the Mien language. How Jim longed for a Christian who could help him translate the Bible! But no Karen could read even if they had the translation.

Young new workers, the Bevingtons, had just arrived and were appointed to the Mien work. But no new workers were on the horizon for the Karen work.

Peter and Jean Nightingale began work with the despised

Akha tribe before there were any Christians among them. But now, with the assistance of Yajoo, a native Akha missionary from Burma, many were turning to Christ. They had formed a Christian village and were helping people break the opium habit. Why didn't God send a native missionary from Burma to help us in the Karen work? Peter reported that a young Akha girl had been shot because she refused to participate in the Akha custom of premarital sex. That was tragic, but, oh how we longed for Karen young people who would have such strong principles and courage for Christ! They reported that the Akha were keen to meet daily for morning and evening devotions. No Karen were even gathering for Sunday worship!

Others reported numbers who attended young people's conferences, believers conferences, and some who attended Bible school. The Akha even had a conference especially to learn how to read music, and now they sang in four-part harmony and wanted instruments to start their own band. All these developments seemed light years ahead of the Karen work where there were no churches and only a handful of believers who had hardly started in the Jesus Way.

Finally it was time for the Karen report. Jim rose and walked slowly to the front. He paused, prayed, then began.

"Just what is OMF's responsibility to the Pwo Karen? For twenty years now OMF has worked among them—first the Carlsons, then the Cookes, next the Hudspiths, and the Murrays. They've all gone on and we're left. We are the only ones on the field who know the Pwo Karen language. We are the only ones who know their culture. Yet years of seed sowing has brought us mostly frustration and disappointment. Are we wasting our time? Are these people too hard for the Lord? Should we move on? Does OMF plan to send more workers, or should we give this responsibility to another mission?"

Jim paused for the group to catch the full impact of that question. Then he went on. "For three years now OMF has had no missionary living among the Pwo. We're at a crossroads with a very difficult decision to make. So I ask you again. What is OMF's responsibility to the Karen? We need your help. What does God want us to do?"

A sober silence fell on the group. Our fellow workers knew how difficult it was to Jim to pose that question. Most of them had been through long periods of waiting for God to work. They knew discouragement, and they weren't going to give shallow advice.

Jim went a bit farther and stuck his neck out. "If OMF keeps the Karen work on, and you agree to get behind it, Louise and I are willing to return to work among them."

I cringed when he said it. Did we really mean it? Was I willing to leave our nice home for the old tribal shack? Were both of us prepared to leave this work among students with all its rewards and go back to the unresponsive Karen people who wanted to use us, but didn't want our God?

The fact that no one else had the language nor the burden to reach these people weighed heavily on us. Others could fill our teaching position in the Thai Bible School, but no one else was prepared to reach the Pwo Karen for Christ. It was an awesome responsibility.

There was a long silence while each field member thought it through. Then they responded. "Yes, we believe you should continue this work among the Pwo Karen. And if you commit yourselves to return, we'll commit ourselves to pray every day for the breakthrough you want to see so badly." Denis Lane picked up the commitment. "Not only will the North Thailand Field pray every day, but so will those in our headquarters in Singapore. We'll lay this need before our whole mission as top priority for prayer this year."

The impact of this decision hit me hard. Would united, persistent prayer make a difference? Did it make sense to leave this beautiful place and strategic work and go back to the unresponsive Karen? Would we receive the same cold, hard rejection as before? Go back to our old tribal shack with the bats and rats—the kerosene lamps and old smoky kerosene refrigerator? Go back to the loneliness, to no mail service, no market and no phone? Go back to the constant demands for medicines—to their ingratitude after we exhausted our time, energy and patience in caring for them? What would our children think? How would Linda feel giving up her newly decorated room?

Yet the unanimous support of our fellow workers confirmed our own call from God that this was right—that God had chosen us to meet this need, that He would fulfill His promises and that He still purposed to call out a people from the Karen tribe as part of the heavenly host from every tribe, tongue and nation who would praise Him for all eternity.

We had no idea how He would fulfill this purpose. We didn't even have assurance that he'd do it in our time. Our job was to be faithful and obedient in telling the Karen in their own language the good news that Jesus was the Living God, that He was stronger than the spirits, and that He loved them and He had opened the way for them to have eternal life. Unless we went, how else could they hear?

# 10
## THE BREAKTHROUGH
### 1974

During the next few weeks as I packed, I kept thinking, if I leave this nice place, surely God will honor my sacrifice and give us a nice place in Karenland. Surely He'll make it up to us. But I had to learn that we can't bargain with God like that. He doesn't owe us anything.

I didn't realize how deeply the bug of materialism had burrowed in my heart. I dreaded exchanging the comforts of Phayao for the old tribal shack in Karenland. Perhaps we could find a nice place in the Thai town of Hod where we could still have electricity and use our appliances. I had forgotten how Abraham got stuck in Haran because of a half-way obedience to God's call.

In March, the hottest and driest time of year in Thailand, we tramped the streets of Hod looking for a house. Hod was a fast-growing centrally located Thai government market town. With our Land-Rover we could easily reach Karen on the plains and in the mountains, and a new bridge over the Ping River gave us quick access to villages on the other side.

After days of empty searching, time was running out. Jim made a deal with a Chinese man to rent a house three miles out of town. When he took me to see it, I hated it. It was an enormous, dark, cavernous barn. Ghastly portraits of the landlord's ancestors peered down at us from the wall. A foreboding picture of a cat watching goldfish swimming in a glass bowl hung on another wall. An ugly mounted ox-head with long horns and bulging glass eyes guarded a doorway. And to top it off, we couldn't use our appliances because the house was just outside the electricity zone.

I felt crushed and physically sick. The truck arrived with our belongings and the driver unceremoniously dumped them in the house. When we began to place the furniture, nothing fit. The couch stuck out into the doorway. The refrigerator covered half a window. The house was filthy, but before we could clean it we had to light the kerosene refrigerator so it would get cold and we could put in the marketing we had brought from the city. Then we set up the butane gas tank and hooked up the stove so we could boil drinking water.

Late that afternoon in the middle of this chaos, some tribal friends arrived to spend the night, and Thai neighbors came over to see what we were doing. It was not a good time for company. As I boiled rice for the tribal folks to eat, the neighbors looked over my shoulder and peppered me with a steady stream of questions. Desperately I prayed, "Lord, if only they would leave me in peace."

The next morning Jim left for two weeks for Singapore to teach a group of new workers, while I stayed to straighten up the mess and settle in. I soon discovered that what we had thought was a quiet Thai neighborhood was the noisiest place we have ever lived. During the night trucks roared down the tiny lane beside our house, revving up their motors to make the steep bank ahead and honking in front of our house to wake up sleeping passengers. The temple across the street blared raucous music and movies into our bedroom window. Gangs of young boys, drunk with rice wine, roamed up and down the street, calling to people and congregating on our front porch to gamble. In worse moments some attempted to crawl up our balcony.

I yearned for our cozy bungalow in Phayao with its view of the lake from the front porch. I thought of friends and family at home with electricity and running water and all the modern comforts. And I grumbled, "Lord, you know what we gave up. Don't we deserve more than this barn? Don't you make any allowances for a woman's desire to make a home?" Again I questioned God's goodness. Had He forgotten us? Did our sacrifices for Him mean nothing?

When Jim returned from Singapore, we began to visit the few Karen Christians scattered on the plains and found much to encourage us. White Sister lived just across the field from our "barn house." She was delighted to see us. Years before, while working in her field, she had whacked a huge cut on her heel with her field knife. We had made many trips to her home to dress the wound and tell her about Jesus. Now she was trusting the Lord. Her brother, Ah Tee, had married one of Boy Jee's daughters and they were also believing. They were excited when we suggested we meet together for worship every Sunday. Boy Jee had moved back down to Sandy Creek area, but he and his family were still believing and were thrilled to have us closer.

When we visited Mrs. Glass and Uncle Silver who now lived in Canaan project, we were amazed to find that five more Karen families had moved down from the mountains to make a new start in Canaan. With great pleasure they assured us that they, along with Mrs. Glass's daughter and husband, were also believing in Jesus. God had been working while we were away. They showed us the big church building the Thai Christians had built in Canaan with Jam Niang, a Thai convert from OMF work in Manorom, as their leader. About 30 people joined a weekend retreat in our "barn house" and enjoyed the fellowship together.

Meanwhile in the mountains, Mrs. Dee was still standing strong in Prosperity Fields. Neighbors had watched when she gathered in her rice by herself. Evidently God-worshippers can grow rice without doing demon worship. They had seen her children get well without making sacrifices to the spirits. They had heard the gospel cassettes she played every Sunday. She was doing well even though she was the only Christian and there were no missionaries were around.

When we drove up the rutted driveway to her house and walked up to her porch she came out of her house beaming from ear to ear.

"Oh, I'm so glad you've come. Two days ago I dreamed you would come today. Some of my neighbors want to believe." She took us inside her house, waved us to sit down on a mat and stirred up the coals in her fireplace. "God has taken good care of me. He answers my prayers. My friends are amazed that I don't do any more demon worship—I just pray and God helps me. They've seen that He is stronger than the spirits. Now they want to turn to Him, too."

She took us to the homes of her friends. Some of them were wives whose husbands were on opium. Three families decided to believe that very day. We helped them burn their demon strings and pray, "Dear God, we believe you are stronger than the spirits. We believe you love us and hear our prayers. We renounce our demon ways and want to follow your way. Please help us in Jesus' name."

When her husband came home from jail she issued him an ultimatum. "If you turn to Christ you can stay here with me, but if you don't turn to Christ you can go live with your other woman." He made a decision to turn to Christ and stay with her.

After sixteen years of working in the field, and only two months after our field members promised to pray daily for us, were we seeing the breakthrough we had prayed for? We were afraid to believe. How many times had we thought we were on the edge? How many times had one person shown interest or a lone person turned? But nothing more had happened. Nothing had developed into a significant turning to Christ.

Just the same we moved up to the Hudspiths' old house for a few weeks and began teaching the new believers and holding

Sunday services. They gathered around the cassette player listening to the same words they had heard so often, but now they seemed to hear with new understanding. Singing was always fun for them. They couldn't read, but they soon memorized the gospel choruses. How they loved the action songs, "Rolled Away" and "The Wise Man Built His House Upon the Rock." Women sang their babies to sleep with "Jesus Loves Me."

Perhaps the best way for them to establish a personal relationship with their new God was to learn how to pray to him. We began with Mrs. White with her broad smile and baby slung in a blanket over one hip.

"I can't pray," she protested. "I don't know the words to say."

"Just talk to God like you would talk to your father," we urged. "Start with 'O Lord God,' then thank him for his love and care, and tell him your needs. Finish your prayer with these words: 'in Jesus' Name, Amen.'

Bravely she began, "O Lord." Then she burst into giggles.

"Go on, go on," the others encouraged. "Keep going. You're doing great!"

She stumbled on and soon was praying without hesitation. Instead of one person leading in prayer, they often wanted everyone to pray at the same time.

Wonder shone on their faces as they listened to Jim explain the big teaching posters. Now was the time to pour Bible stories into their minds—stories about Jesus and his power to change lives. His power to change the tax collector from a greedy man to a generous man. His power to forgive the prostitute's sins. His power to cast a legion of demons out of the wild man of the Gesarenes. His power over the forces of nature when he calmed the storm. The stories began to give them a brand new idea of God's love and power. He was stronger than the spirits.

Along with the Bible stories came basic instructions for personal hygiene—take baths with soap, drink boiled water, eat good food, avoid eating raw meat and use a mosquito net.

Every day they came with their sicknesses, asking for medicine. The results of putting lotion on scabies, taking medicines for worms and malaria, and daily vitamins soon made them look like different people—bright eyes, clean faces with color in their cheeks.

One day a child appeared at the porch with a suspicious rash, and soon a measles epidemic swept through the village. Many families were prostrated on their porches, too weak to work or even cook rice to eat. We were called from home to home to help people with medicines and had many opportunities to show loving care by washing a feverish face or offering a nourishing drink.

We soon got to know several families, including Song Paw's. Song Paw worked for a week clearing up his opium business and burning sacrificial fetishes in his field to get rid of the lord spirit of the land, the lord spirit of the water and the lord spirit of rice. God was the true Lord of these things, not an evil spirit. By Sunday of that week he was ready to turn to Christ. Even while thunder rolled and his children coughed with bronchitis, he bravely cut off his demon strings and destroyed the demon house he had built to protect his family house from a nearby tree that had been struck by lightning.

When the porch became too small, the new believers gathered materials to build a meeting place. They carried in posts from the jungle, and peeled and trimmed them with their field knives. They split and flattened bamboo poles to use for walls and soaked them in the creek until all the bugs were killed. They gathered broad leaves from the jungle and wove them into shingles for roofing. When a group of Chinese Christians in Singapore heard about the new believers, they sent money to buy wooden boards for the floor. When materials were all ready, the Karen believers gathered together and put up the structure in one day. Everyone pitched in to help. Men dug deep holes in the ground to put in the posts. Even the women helped saw floor boards to make them even. The first church in

Prosperity Fields took shape and stood firmly as a visible, tangible monument that God had returned. He was here in Karenland. About 30 people attended Sunday worship.

Early on these new believers learned the hard way that they must respect the Lord's Day. Trying to help them find ways of earning extra money, we brought some bars of brass from the city so that Mr. Dee could make Karen bracelets to sell. He was so excited about doing this that he began pounding on them as soon as we gave them to him, not even stopping to attend Sunday morning service. While the service was being held in the church we saw him on his porch, bent over his anvil, and pounding with his hammer. Suddenly he groaned and clutched his stomach. He had such terrible cramps he had to stop working on the bracelets. After the service ended he pleaded for medicine and soon recovered, but he had learned that Sunday was the Lord's Day. He had to make time for God first, and not put his personal work before God's business.

More and more Karen began turning in the mountains. God had broken through in answer to prayer and was working in a way we had never known before. It was certainly beyond our doing. People were turning from villages we had never visited. A movement of His Spirit had truly begun.

# 11
## TESTING
### 1974

The Tyrant does not easily let go his prey. When Karen people turned to Christ from demons, we warned them, "It won't always be easy. Sickness, social pressure, failed crops—Satan will use all of these and many more tricks to turn you away from Jesus."

Mrs. Dee's neighbor, Mrs. Bite, was a demon priestess in Prosperity Fields, and when she turned away from the demon spirits, she knew what she had to do. She surrendered the special bag holding the dagger used to kill the sacrificial pigs and the old black pot used for cooking the rice for the offerings. The new Christians were afraid even to touch this powerful paraphernalia for fear the demons would take revenge on them. By this time Mr. Dee had become Jim's right-hand man, learning how to pray and help people turn to the Lord. With much prayer, Mr. Dee helped Jim burn Mrs. Bite's demon things.

Mrs. Bite's testimony was so compelling that two of her daughters and their husbands also believed. One daughter, 21-year-old White Star, was a quiet beautiful girl with a year-old baby. Her husband was a tribal man from Burma where many of the Karen are believers.

We had met White Star and treated her when she became ill with measles, but now she seemed well and very certain that she wanted to follow Jesus. "Even if I die, I still want to believe in Jesus," she told us with deep conviction.

We were still living on the plains when this happened. One day Grandpa Waters appeared suddenly at our door. We knew something was wrong to cause the old man to make the long trip down from the mountain. He had not believed himself, but he told us, "One of your people has died."

Who was it? What had happened? We tried to pull the story out of him. "She got very bad diarrhea yesterday," he went on, "and no matter what we did, she got worse. In a few hours she died. We knew the spirits would take revenge. Her mother is head of her demon clan—she is too powerful to believe in Jesus." As he blurted out the story bit by bit, we realized it must be White Star.

We got in the Land-Rover with Grandpa Waters and headed up to Prosperity Fields, wondering what we'd find and how we could comfort this poor mother. She had never heard of Job's trials. She didn't know about the spiritual battle described in Ephesians. She had no Scriptures in which to find hope. Were the evil spirits really taking revenge? Why did Jesus allow them to take the life of this beautiful girl? Why didn't He answer their prayers and heal this new believer? If He is stronger than the Strong Man, why did He not keep this young believer from dying?

Along the ridge road to Omkoy we met Boy Jee. It was most unusual for Boy Jee to come this far from his home in Sandy Creek, but here he was, walking along the road with two baskets of piglets he planned to sell. We stopped, told him the story, and asked him if he'd come with us. "You might be able to help," we told him. God had tested Boy Jee soon after his baptism when his baby girl had hydroencephalitis. No medicine helped her, and to make it worse, the neighbors teased

Boy Jee and his wife about their "Jesus baby." "This is what happens to people who leave the demons and turn to Christ," they said. The little girl lived to about five years, and then she died. But Boy Jee was assured in a vivid dream that she was now in heaven, safe and happy with Jesus, and one day he would be reunited with her

When we arrived in the village the situation was even worse than Grandpa Waters had told us. Trust in Jesus had been shattered by this tragic event. White Star had been weakened by measles, then she ate some bad mangoes and developed severe food poisoning. The symptoms developed so rapidly and so severely they had no time to call for help. The believers prayed, but when White Star became worse instead of better, Mr. Dee, who should have taken a strong lead, was so petrified with fear that he ran away. Nothing they did would halt the disease and she died that night.

To make matters worse, another demon priestess in the same village had a daughter about the same age who had the same symptoms. This demon priestess did demon worship for her daughter and her daughter got well. How could we explain that to the new Christians? Where was God? Was He really stronger than the demons, as we had so often told them? Why hadn't He intervened? What could we say to them now? Would Mrs. Bite turn back to the demons?

That's when Boy Jee began to comfort and counsel the family. "Don't go back to the demon way, Mother!" he urged. "Your daughter is with Jesus. Keep trusting him and you'll see your daughter again someday in heaven. I, too, had a daughter that died," he went on. "But I know she is with Jesus and that someday I'll see her again."

Boy Jee's words stirred a chord deep down inside Mrs. Bite's heart. Yes, even Christians die. But her daughter was with Jesus. She had said, "Even if I die, I want to believe in Jesus." Somehow a spark of heavenly hope was born in that mother's grieving heart. She didn't have to fear that her daughter's ghost was roaming around bothering living people. This is not the end. God is in heaven preparing a place for his own people. A ray of hope in eternal life that was more valuable than life on earth suddenly shone into the darkness of that hour. God, who commanded light to drive out darkness, was beginning to show the Pwo Karen people His glory and power in a more lasting way. He is stronger, even in death.

Non-Christians couldn't understand what kept Mrs. Bite from going back to the demons. "Why does she continue to worship a God who had failed her so miserably?" they asked. Those who wanted to jump on the bandwagon of easy believism were sifted out. Those who chose to follow Christ had to face the fact that God was sovereign. He cannot be manipulated by a push-button prayer. His ways are far superior to our ways. We wanted with all our hearts to protect these young weak believers, but He had his plan and process in training them to be strong in the faith. Mrs. Bite chose to continue to follow God's Way.

Thinking back, our big test had come when we lived in Sandy Creek. Jim was away on a trek and I was home alone with four-month-old Kevin and two-year-old Linda. During the night I noticed that Linda was jerking spasmodically. I reached for her and realized she was not feverish, but was having a convulsion. I held her for what seemed a long time but was probably only a minute or so until she relaxed into a deep sleep. The next day I took her to see a doctor in Chiangmai. After a week of tests the doctors told us that the x-ray of her skull showed intercranial pressure, which could mean a brain tumor. They advised us to take her home to the States immediately. We didn't have enough money for all of us to go, so Jim took her to Kansas while I stayed with Kevin in Chiangmai.

When I placed Linda in Jim's arms, I didn't know if I would see her alive again. Still, God gave me deep peace. Many people around the world prayed, and, in an amazing way God took care of air transportation, finances, and many other details for that trip. A neurosurgeon in Kansas checked Linda thoroughly and found nothing abnormal.

Two weeks after Jim and Linda left, I received a telegram. "Happy Valentine's Day! Linda is clear. Coming home next week." I could hardly believe it! Three weeks after the attack we were back together again, thankful God had spared our little girl.

All these thoughts crowded my mind as we tried to minister to Mrs. Bite and to those believers who loved White Star. Testing, we knew, was part of the spiritual battle they'd have to endure. Satan tries to pull us away from our faith, put doubts in our minds about God's gracious character and stop our witness. But He is sovereign. He chose to take Mrs. Bite's and Boy Jee's daughters and to spare ours. How we longed to protect these new believers, even as we realized that testing would lead to the strengthening of their faith. These were his children, not ours. He would hold on to them.

The Karen believers often saw God answer prayer. A lady who had sick chickens prayed that God would make them well, and she was very excited when He did. Later, however, when her chickens were sick again, she prayed the same prayer expecting God to answer in the same way, but that time He chose not to heal her chickens.

"Oh-oh," she reasoned. "Something's wrong. God didn't answer my prayer. Have I offended Him? Is He angry with me, like the demons get angry? Should I appease Him the way I used to appease the demons?"

She and the others had deep lessons to learn, and we tried to explain. God isn't angry, but neither is He a prayer vending machine. He has greater purposes in mind. His ways are higher than our ways. He doesn't promise to keep our chickens or us healthy. He has promised, however, to be there for us when we're sick and when our chickens are sick. He may do that in a way we don't understand or expect, but we must continue to trust His loving care and good intentions for us.

Mang Jo had a different lesson to learn. He could have finished his rice harvest on Sunday, but he decided to keep the Lord's Day and go with us to help some new families turn. As his newly cut rice lay drying in the field, a torrential downpour flooded the narrow mountain valley and swept away one-third of his crop. We had just taught him how God created all things and was in total control of nature.

"Then why doesn't He stop the rain from ruining my crop?" It was especially hard for him, so new in the Christian life and not being able to read God's Word for comfort and encouragement in such trials. But Mang Jo didn't give in to pressure to turn back to the demon way, and as the year went on God supplied his need.

When Song Paw's family got sick, he led Jim out to his field house where his wife and children sat huddled together on a mat shivering with fever.

"What's gone wrong?" he asked us. "I believed in Jesus and yet my wife and family all became sick. You told us God is stronger than the spirits. So why aren't they all well?"

Those are hard questions to answer. Yes, God is powerful. He does have more power than the spirits, but he doesn't remove all sickness and trouble from Christians. In the past all their former spirit worship centered around making the spirits happy so that they would keep physically well. Now it's difficult for them to learn this further lesson of maturity in the new Christian way and to understand that God is still God and worthy of our worship whether in sickness or in health. We can trust Him in good times and in bad. He sees a larger picture and gives us hope.

Song Paw was sorely tempted to turn back, but Jim prayed with him and encouraged him to hang on in faith to God. "God knows and God cares. He'll help you."

He did hang on, and eventually Song Paw's family became better physically and he grew stronger spiritually.

# 12
## TURNING IN
## STRIPED CREEK
### 1975

We were still living in Hod, down on the plains, making regular forays to Prosperity Fields when the breakthrough came. Our old house in Striped Creek was still standing, primitive as it was, although no one in that village had yet turned to the Lord. We couldn't forget that time and time again the people in that village had rejected the gospel, in the face of God's power. Still, we wanted to be there in the mountains where it seemed to us that the Spirit was moving. The Christians on the plains were disappointed when they learned we were leaving, but they could find other believers at the church in Canaan if they wanted to make the effort, and we would visit them from time to time.

Most of the furniture we had used before in Striped Creek— a cupboard with screen doors, a folding table and chairs, bamboo stools, a dresser and bed—was still there. So we packed the big old mission furniture we had used in Hod and sent it on a truck back to Chiangmai. I was glad to see it go. Then, every time we made a trip to the mountains we packed the Land-Rover with dishes, linens, some new mats to put around the firebox, a big clay pot for storing rain water, and new posters of the Good Shepherd seeking the lost lamb and the Two Ways to replace the old tattered ones on the walls. We didn't put up curtains because the Karen kids had used them to wipe their noses.

The old shack with the straw thatched roof and all its dust and mold hadn't improved with age. The fresh bamboo smell had faded long ago. Now it was weather-beaten, musty, black from smoky fires, and inhabited by bats. Rats had chewed into the dresser drawer leaving a dirty nest and droppings. The walls were dusty, the floor sagged, and the old linoleum was pitted with mildew. But the bats and the rats didn't matter anymore. This was our home, and it was good to be back. We cleaned it up, laid down new shelf paper, even kept the dresser the rats had chewed.

A deep joy and peace welled up in our hearts as we sat on our wooden benches at the kitchen table. We were so happy and busy with people who were turning to God after all the years of waiting. God had changed our hearts. This was where we were needed, where He wanted us to do His work. Be it ever so humble, this was our home. We lit the kerosene lamp, dusted off the old table and sat down on straw mats by the fire. Great peace flooded our hearts. This was God's place for us. A nice home and beautiful furniture wasn't that important after all.

Geekay and his family still lived near our house. When we lived in Striped Creek the first time he had been our closest friend. When he plowed his fields, planted his rice, and harvested, he took Jim along and carefully explained the meaning of each step in the process and each ceremony.

For hours after supper each night, he sat by our fire and helped Jim with the language. He told Karen legends which Jim recorded, and then they spent hours poring over the tapes to help Jim understand.

In turn Jim answered all Geekay's questions about America and about our foreign customs. Then he told him Bible stories. Sometimes Geekay was interested, but he had gone the old spirit way for so long, it was difficult for him to even think of anything else. Besides, he wondered, maybe this white man was spinning a yarn to make a good story, just like the Karen did. That resurrection story, for instance—did Jesus really rise from the dead, or was that the same magic that Karen tell about in their fairy tales?

Geekay had admitted the demons hadn't helped him. He told us about his three-year-old son. One day Geekay was going to a village about an hour away. His son wanted to go along, but Geekay said no, picked up his shoulder bag and started down the trail. He didn't realize that the boy was following him. Geekay walked quickly, and soon the little boy lost sight of him. Only when Geekay returned home did he find out that the boy had followed him and hadn't returned.

The villagers searched the jungle, and Geekay ran back along the path he had taken. Others fanned out on different trails to hunt for the little one. They searched for three days before they finally gave up. Three months later they found the child's bones and concluded that the demons must have hid him. "We searched right on this very spot," they said, "and we didn't see him!" No wonder Geekay was angry with the demons!

Geekay had observed how medicines and prayer had helped sick people. His own teenaged daughter had been so sick that she could only lie on her porch. She gratefully accepted the medicine we offered her and finally recovered. Geekay knew others who had refused the medicine and had died. Later when his daughter again became very ill with terrible stomach pains, Geekay decided to take a step closer. He asked Jim to pray and give medecine to his daughter and he wouldn't do demon worship. For four days we prayed and treated her, watching anxiously for God to work. Finally she began to recover. Geekay was happy that he didn't waste a pig making a sacrifice for her, but still he hadn't turned to Christ.

The gospel has to meet people where they feel a need. Medicine was one place they felt a need. Having enough rice to eat was another. Could God provide rice? Rice is extremely important to Karen. "Even God has to eat rice," Geekay told Jim.

When Jim told him he had grown up without eating rice, Geekay could hardly believe it. "If we Karen people didn't eat rice we would soon die. We have to eat rice every day, but my field is so small I don't get enough rice to last even half a year."

"If you want more rice, you have to plant more," Jim told him. "God is Creator of the world. He created rice. He created the ground it grows in and the water and the sun that causes it to grow. Look where rain comes from—from heaven. God sends it. He's the one who makes rice grow." Geekay's father and grandfather had always worshiped spirits whenever they planted rice. They sacrificed many chickens for just one field. Yes, Geekay thought, the demon way was making them poorer. Maybe the Jesus way would be better, but how could a Karen possibly grow rice only by praying to Jesus without making any sacrifices to demons? Can Jesus really make rice grow? He had never been really convinced.

When Karen Christians came to visit us, Geekay heard them sing Jesus songs and pray. Around the fire at night he asked them, "Can Christians really grow rice in their fields without doing demon worship?"

They assured him, "Yes, God can grow rice."

So one year when the time came to plant his fields, Geekay decided he wouldn't do the usual ceremonies. He'd just ask Jim to pray. That year his field grew as well as anyone else's. This was good, but Geekay still could not step out and make a decision to follow Jesus. How could he go against all the other Karen people? Just before harvest his son-in-law did some demon ceremonies for the field, but Geekay had seen enough with his own eyes to convince him that God could make rice grow. He was coming closer, but he had never made that definite step of commitment.

After we moved back to Striped Creek and Jim told Geekay about the new Christians in Prosperity Fields, Geekay decided to see for himself. He and his wife went to the Thanksgiving service for the new Christians in Prosperity Fields, and he was surprised to see so many Karen believers bringing the first fruits of their harvest as offerings—bags of rice, yellow pumpkins, green marrows, red peppers. If others were taking that step, he could, too. "Bring Boy Jee with you next week," he told Jim, "I'm going to turn to Jesus."

The next Sunday Boy Jee and Jim helped Geekay burn the demon things in his house. Boy Jee cut the strings off Geekay's wrists and off the wrists of each member of his family as we sang "Jesus has won the victory over Satan."

Soon Geekay and Jim began translating the book of Mark into Pwo Karen. What a difference it made to work with a Christian! As Geekay soaked in the Word he grew stronger in his faith, and he asked to be baptized. He'd seen other Christians baptized and wanted to follow in that step of obedience before we left for furlough. So we walked down to his new field by a small stream, and Geekay, his wife, their son, Note, and our son Nathan were all baptized.

Geekay's problems didn't go away when he turned to Jesus. People in Striped Creek talked against him. A friend who promised to turn at the same time backed out the last minute. Even relatives turned against them. Geekay's wife now sat alone in her house because her relative's child died and they blamed the death on her because she had left the demons. Geekay's two sons were angry that their parents had turned because it lessened their chances to find a good wife.

Geekay had the gifts and heart to lead the Christian group in Striped Creek, but he faced some difficult tests. Opium was an increasing problem among the Pwo Karen. They don't usually grow opium, but they smoke it, and when young boys go through the ritual of becoming men, they are given opium to dull the pain of tattooing. They are tattooed from knee to waist, and the process takes two days—one day for each leg. They still feel pain as the blunt stylus jabs through the outer skin to the sensitive inner layer and deposits a blue-black ink made from bear organs. Some die in this ordeal.

"Why do you go through this pain?" we asked.

"Oh, we do it out of respect for our mothers who suffered in childbirth for us. And, of course, we do it so the girls will like us."

Some of the young men stay hooked on opium when they learn that it also blots out the pain, the drudgery, and the boredom of life. When the occasional smoke grows into a bad habit, the smoker turns into a criminal and steals things in order to get opium. Or, he becomes a slave to the Hmong tribesmen who grow opium as a cash crop. Men sell fields, elephants, livestock, houses all for the sake of getting some opium to smoke. Tribal justice is swift and final. If an addict is caught stealing buffalo he is warned several times and finally killed if he doesn't reform. They usually wait along a trail on a dark night and shoot the opium smoker.

Geekay's friend, Jee Bout, was a smart man, but was heavily addicted to opium. The Headman warned Jee Bout that the villagers considered him a menace, and if he didn't quit smoking they would get rid of him. Geekay felt sorry for Jee Bout and urged him to turn to Jesus. "He is stronger than the evil spirits," he told Jee Bout. He can help you break with opium. It's worth a try—otherwise you're dead!"

Geekay's brother-in-law, Paht Gahng, faced the same problem. Geekay helped both families, including wives and children, to pray and burn their demon things. Next Jee Bout moved his house next door to Geekay, and Geekay took both men down to his field house to break the habit. They quit for a time, but soon both men were back on the pipe.

We had been on furlough, and when we returned, we found that four families in Striped Creek had turned to Christ: Geekay's family, his daughter and her family, and the two opium addicts and their families. About twenty gathered for Sunday services, and sometimes met in the evenings for times of singing. Other missionaries had cared for and encouraged them while we were gone. The new believers helped Jim put up a meeting place, some of younger children began learning to read, and the church in Striped Creek took on a visible form.

Geekay, however, was deeply disappointed. He felt that his prayers weren't powerful enough to help his friends break with opium. We took the two addicts into our home to try again to break the habit. We gave full time attention to them—nursed them, fed them vitamins, gave them hot drinks and sleeping medicine, and prayed with them when the craving became worse. To keep them occupied we bought bars of brass for them to pound into bracelets and sell. They did well for a short time, but when the pain was bad, their wives felt sorry for them and secretly gave them a bit of opium.

We were all disappointed when they slipped back and the joy faded from their faces. Geekay was most disappointed—not only in the men, but in God. If he couldn't help his friends, Geekay felt as if he didn't have God's power to be a leader to his own people. Villagers who were watching concluded that the Jesus Way is no different; it can't change opium smokers.

It was a hard lesson for Geekay. It's God's work, not ours. He is the leader, and as we work with Him in telling others about Christ we constantly face the triangle of God's will, our will, and also the will of the person we are working with. God does not force anyone. That person has the right to choose which way he will go.

Geekay had other lessons to learn as well. He still did not have enough rice from his fields, but one day he heard that a man wanted to sell some excellent rice fields.

"These fields are cursed by a very powerful demon," the man lamented. "Every time we plant the fields someone in our family gets sick and dies. We must get rid of them, even though they are excellent fields."

Geekay thought of his little field which was often flooded and washed by stones, so he went to Jim, "Does God really have more power than the spirits?"

"He certainly does," Jim assured him.

"I don't have money to buy fields, but maybe I could trade

my small fields for his big fields," Geekay figured.

The man agreed to trade, and Geekay and Jim went to pray for the cursed fields, asking God to help Geekay grow good rice without anyone in his family dying.

Geekay worked hard because the fields were large, and the first year he got a very good crop. At harvest time Geekay took us down to see, and we took a picture of him posing with his first fruits: a giant cucumber in one hand and a sheaf of ripe grain in the other. Surely, he thought, this would impress others in Striped Creek, but they told him, "Oh, one year doesn't prove any thing. You have to get a good crop for three years!"

The second year Geekay suddenly collapsed with a bleeding ulcer. We rushed him to Chiangmai hospital, thinking, that he was too far gone to help. But a doctor quickly inserted an intravenous drip into Geekay's leg, and he revived. God had answered prayer again. The family harvested a good crop and no one died. And the same for the third year. To these new Christians who had lived so long in a world of evil spirits, it was another evidence that Jesus was stronger than the Strong Man who had kept them prisoner so long.

# 13

## BUFFALO VILLAGE TO
## FLOATING FIELDS

The word began to spread quickly now from village to village. Sometimes we had no idea how they heard. One Sunday morning Jim, in his red Karen tunic and stocking feet, was preaching to the Christians in Prosperity Fields. The congregation sat on mats on the wooden floor of their open-sided church building, listening intently. There was so much for new believers to learn.

Suddenly there was a commotion at the back of the church and everyone turned to look. A man and his wife staggered up the ladder into the church, each carrying a child wrapped in a blanket, hot and soaking wet with sweat and rain.

"We're from Buffalo Village, and we've come to turn to Jesus. We're sick and want medicines, so we are going to become Christians."

I groaned! Another case of believing in Jesus just so they can be healed without understanding what Christ's death on the cross means! I'd never seen this family before. We had never even been to Buffalo Village. Still, they had heard about Jesus, and had walked twenty miles in the rain to hear more.

"Please wait until the meeting is over and then we will tend to your needs," Jim told them.

Later their story unfolded. They had been working in a new rice field when their four older children became desperately sick with fever and died. They consulted a demon priest who told them the field was cursed. When they worked the field, the demons had become very angry and had killed their children. The demons also threatened to kill the two younger children and themselves. Now U Vang and his wife were trying desperately to save their own lives and their two remaining children. How could they escape? They heard that Jesus was stronger than the evil spirits and they determined to find him.

No wonder they were desperate! I felt rebuked for having misjudged them. And I thought of people who often questioned us. "Why do you want to change the tribal people? Why not leave them in their pristine state?" Certainly here was a clear case: if these people remained in their present state, Satan would eventually destroy them. The two children had high fevers, so we treated them and their parents for malaria, and they recovered and turned to Jesus.

When U Vang and his family returned to Buffalo Village, they told his brother what Jesus had done for them and how he had defeated Satan on the cross. The brother and his family all turned to the Lord along with several neighbors. Only Jesus, they realized, could free them from the powerful curse of the demons.

Meanwhile, down on the plains, God was still working to show that He was stronger than the demons. A Karen man from the plains came to see us in Striped Creek. "Please come help my wife. She is dying."

"What's the matter with your wife?" we asked.

"She can't eat rice."

"What do you mean, she can't eat rice?"

"She can't swallow. She was sick, so the demon priest divined and told us to do a certain demon ceremony. He said my wife can't swallow rice until we sacrifice the newly hatched chickens from a certain hen. But while we were doing this, the baby cried, so the ceremony didn't work, and we have to do it over again."

"So, why don't you get another chicken and do it again?" Jim asked.

"Oh, Jo Dee, that's the trouble. It has to be a chicken from this same hen. We have to wait until she lays another batch of eggs and then hatches them. That will take at least three more weeks. Meanwhile my wife can't swallow rice, and if she can't eat rice for three weeks she'll die!"

Oh, I thought, the tyranny of the Evil One! How he ties up these people in knots to perform every meticulous detail of his imperious orders! How he laughs when they have done everything so carefully and it still doesn't work! He's a cruel taskmaster.

We weren't able to go down to see this lady, but Jim prayed for her, asking that Satan would flee and that God would release her throat so she could swallow rice.

"Now go and feed your wife some rice," he told the man.

Later we learned that the lady recovered and flourished, and when the family saw how God had delivered them from the power of the curse, they all turned to Jesus.

One day we visited Floating Fields, one of the largest Karen villages in the mountains. Golden rays from the October sun filtered over the narrow mountain valley, and the hills nearby cast afternoon shadows on the recently harvested rice fields. Puffing and sweating from hiking all day, we left the quiet pine forest and followed the trail through a patch of weeds higher than our heads and finally emerged into a golden valley. Across the valley bamboo huts perched on the mountainside with smoke curling out of their pointed grass roof tops. Women were cooking rice for supper.

Suddenly, right there in the middle of the jungle, the trail became a two-track road. Our Karen guide explained: "Headman Beng Vang saw Thai people on the plains using ox-carts, so he made one for himself to carry in his rice from the fields." Surely this was the first ox-cart a Karen ever made! We realized that this Beng Vang must be a clever man and worthy of respect.

That night we stayed in Beng Vang's home. Having just harvested his crop, he had plenty of rice, and while women busily prepared food over the smoky fire, the men sat cross-legged on the open porch smoking pipes and plying us with questions about that wonderland, America.

"Is it true you can't walk from this country to that country?"

"Do people grow rice in America?"

Finally, Mrs. Beng Vang called, "Food's ready! Come eat!"

We sat on the floor around a low round table, and Mrs. Beng Vang placed steaming mounds of pink-colored mountain rice on a black lacquered tray beside a bowl of peppery pumpkin stew. We ate the rice with our fingers and took turns using the one enamel spoon to throw stew into our mouths.

No one stopped to thank God for the food, of course. They didn't know the God who made rice grow and gave them strength to prepare it. They only knew the fearful way of demon worship, and Beng Vang was tired of it. He looked at his arms and body covered with tattoos which were supposed to protect him from evil spirits. Grimy strings circled his wrists. He seemed to be endlessly sacrificing to spirits.

Recently a peddler had come by offering injections of medicine, claiming they would protect him from evil spirits. Beng Vang paid a pretty price for a shot, but instead of feeling better he came down with a raging fever and chills. The injection was useless. Nearly dead, he resorted to demon worship and was just now recovering. No more medicine for him, he vowed, but he despaired how he'd ever break free from the evil spirits.

Now here was this white man saying that Jesus is stronger than the demons. He can deliver us from their power. He is the God who created us. In the beginning our forefathers worshiped him, but they forgot his way and sacrificed to the spirits instead. Still, He loves us and wants us to come back to Him. Beng Vang listened intently as the truth sank into his heart. Here was a way to be free from the power of evil spirits.

The next time we saw Beng Vang, he had moved from

Floating Fields to begin a new village in the jungle. He was starting over from scratch, clearing the land and digging out stumps. One day as he hacked down a tree with his razor sharp knife he cut off his thumb. Grabbing the stump with his remaining four fingers he checked the bleeding and carried on until the job was done.

We were having a meeting in the new church at Prosperity Fields when a message arrived: "Beng Vang orders you to come to his village. He wants to believe." A group of Christians from Prosperity Fields piled into our Land-Rover and we started over the terrible road. Fallen pine trees blocked the way. Old culverts had been washed out by heavy rains. Several times the Land-Rover nearly tipped over trying to straddle deep ruts. We turned off on a winding road which Beng Vang had slashed through the jungle until we came to a clearing. His home was on stilts, large and cool in the middle of a big yard circled by a wooden rail fence. Pigs rooted in the yard; chickens picked under his porch. All his tools hung neatly on the wall inside his house. Weaving equipment, loom and spinning wheel, sat in one corner. Underneath the house stood an anvil and forge where this innovative man made knives out of an old car spring. We marveled at his ingenuity. If he lived in our country, we thought, he'd be working for NASA.

"Come see my sugar cane press," he urged us. He had carved gears out of teak wood to press the sugar cane. Sweet juice ran out, which he poured into a huge wok sitting over an outdoor fire and boiled until it was thick. Then he poured the molten mass onto a clean bamboo mat to harden into sheets of brown sugar. He cut these into blocks, wrapping each section with a broad leaf from the jungle and tying it with a bamboo strip. It would keep like that for months.

Beng Vang's eldest daughter and her opium-smoking husband lived nearby with four small children. She and Youngest Daughter, beautiful and graceful, helped their mother prepare a meal while Beng Vang told us about his family. "Our oldest son, Jo Gate, lives near our old home. Son Gleck, here, has a crippled leg, but a good mind. A witch doctor told me the spirits were angry because I got that injection to get rid of the demons, so they made his leg lame." Gleck would never be strong enough to work fields. Dae, the youngest son, sat on a back step, scowling. He wasn't sure about these foreigners and their new way.

When we sat down to eat, Jim thanked God for the rice and soup. I needed that grace when I saw the fat, white, pleated grub worms floating on top of the soup; others considered them a delicacy.

After the meal we sang hymns and Jim explained the gospel message from the poster roll. These big pictures showed how sin, like a deep chasm, separated us from God. But the cross of Jesus bridged this chasm. If we believe in Jesus and ask him to save us, he takes our sins away and we can come back to God and become his children.

Beng Vang, his wife and two sons repeated after him, "Greatest God, we have followed the demon way. Now we want to follow your way. Please forgive us our sins and help us to follow you." The two daughters and their husbands watched, but they didn't commit themselves yet. While one of the believers who had come with us took bits of feathers and bamboo fetishes down from the door, Jim pulled his knife out of his pocket and slit the spirit strings off their wrists and necks. Next they broke a long pole which they used for calling back the spirits. When all these emblems of spirit worship were gathered up, we made a bonfire outside, burned them and sang, "Jesus has conquered Satan; Praise His name."

Now began the slow, difficult process of helping them turn from the old way and learn to walk in the new one. The next morning Beng Vang was on our doorstep with his son who was still weak after three months of malaria fever. Sacrifices to the demons had not helped him. Now that he was a Christian he would see if God's way worked better. A Christian friend took him to Maesariang clinic where he recovered.

Months later when Beng Vang's wife became ill, he called

us to come take her to the hospital. We suggested she try antacid pills first, but they weren't satisfied until we drove her to the hospital. After a long and expensive trip the doctor told us she only needed antacid pills for her stomach. They had no idea how much time and money was involved to take them that far, but they were so fearful of sickness and expected us to cure all their aches and pains because they were now Christians.

Once again Beng Vang called Jim down to his village for a feast and asked him to pray especially for his children. They discussed the new way, but Beng Vang couldn't understand why Christians still got sick. In the old way evil spirits caused sickness. How can eating insufficient food or wrong food cause disease? Jim tried to explain. "If I put water in my Land-Rover, it won't go very far. I have to put gas in so it will run. We have to eat and put the right kind of food into our bodies so we'll have strength to work."

Beng Vang watched his little granddaughter splashing and smiling at us while she took her bath in a pig trough. "Sometimes she has fits." The doctor diagnosed her as having epilepsy. She would need to take medicine all her life. Beng Vang couldn't understand why she didn't get well after a few doses of medicine. It was a hard lesson, learning to trust God all the way, through good times and bad times, when he answers prayer and when those prayers seemed to go unanswered. God knows what is best and is working out his purposes to strengthen our faith.

Son Gleck, too, felt unhappy when he wasn't instantly free from all sickness. He tried to go back to the demon ways. He began to prepare the two pigs for sacrifice, but in the process he cut himself. That canceled the sacrifice and he had to start all over again with another two pigs. Again he cut himself. Finally he decided wasting six pigs was too much. He came back to God's way and learned to read. His mind was so keen that in three days he could read anything written in his own language. Like most Karen he loved to sing and began strumming hymn tunes on his homemade harp.

Beng Vang and Son Gleck made a strong father-son team. The father was too old to learn to read, but nevertheless he commanded great respect for his wisdom and experience. He explained the poster pictures while Gleck read and sang. Together they made a tape telling how they had turned to God, and singing a song they had composed about the new way.

All Beng Vang's children turned to Christ including his oldest son, Jo Gate, who turned to Christ in another village along with several other families. Beng Vang decided to be baptized, so he called Jim to come. The two Christian men, Dee Waters and Geekay, helped baptize them in a deep spot in the creek, bordered with brilliant orange azaleas. Afterwards, back up at the house, Beng Vang gave thanks to God for providing our chicken and rice meal. A service followed and then communion. As we received the emblems of the Lord's supper—rice in a bowl and water from a battered tin cup—from the hands of Karen Christians, we felt drawn together as members of God's family. God's grace working in the lives of these Karen was truly awesome!

One day we visited Beng Vang and found him very discouraged. His cows had been lost for two weeks. "If God knows everything and can do everything, why doesn't He show us where those cows are?"

"Have you prayed about it?" we asked.

"Of course! We've prayed and prayed and prayed! God must not care about us any more!" We tried to encourage him, but our words seemed empty. We sang and read the Bible even though the heavens seemed like brass. But during our final prayer Beng Vang looked up and saw his lost cows walk past the open door. God was still alive and well! He had heard and answered prayer. His timing was perfect.

# 14

## 200 BABIES IN OUR NURSERY
## 1975-1979

T he good news that Jesus was stronger than the spirits spread far and wide as Christians told relatives and neighbors how Christ had helped them. Besides Prosperity Fields and Striped Creek, groups of Christians now met regularly in Big Water, Dusty, Grass, Vine, Hope, Mine and Buffalo villages, with one or two scattered families in several other villages.

Much work, however, lay ahead to get these infant churches established. We believed the new church should be as Pwo Karen as possible but, of course, without demon worship. For example, the Karen love to sing, and the few hymns Joe Cooke had written using indigenous tunes were tremendously popular, but we needed more. Jim can't carry a tune, but he has a good sense of rhyme and rhythm. He translated some of our old favorite hymns and packed them full of doctrine, so that as Karen sang them they stored God's truth in their minds and hearts. Often we heard mothers singing their babies to sleep with "Holy, Holy, Holy" or "How Great Thou Art."

We also needed Scriptures, so Jim and Geekay worked on Mark, Acts, and John, but they were often interrupted with other pressing needs. The new believers needed to learn to read so they could read God's Word for themselves. We started them memorizing the alphabet chart on our wall, while some of the younger missionaries who had joined us spent long, painstaking hours teaching them to read from the primers. When the Karen first picked up a book, they didn't even know how to hold it. We even had to teach them which was the right side up, which was the front, and how to work, page by page, from the front to the back.

It took them a long time to understand that a drawing on a page represented something real.

"What's that?" they'd ask.

"A pig."

They'd look puzzled. Those black and white line drawings on the page didn't look like the pig that lived under their house. Sometimes the thought of how much they had to learn was overwhelming, and it was at those times we realized that God would care for them. He promised that His spirit would enlighten their darkened minds and give them understanding.

We made a series of the main Bible stories from Genesis to the second coming, using a simple line drawing on one page with a caption underneath and a short explanation on the opposite page. We pasted these pages on our wall, and the new Christians memorized the captions while the pictures jogged their memory of a story we had told them. When they finished reading the primers, they practiced more reading in these Bible story books. By the time they finished this series they could begin to read the newly translated book of Mark.

Nathan, who was about five at the time, was a great help in motivating the Karen to read. Every night he crawled into my lap and begged me to read to him. The Karen learned quickly by watching us that we valued reading. Nathan even learned to read the Karen primers and taught his little friends. One time, his small friend, while chewing a mouthful of betel nut, didn't make it to the window in time and dribbled red betel juice all over the new set of flash cards I had worked on for two days. How he managed to hit every card, I'll never know. I shook my head in wonder as I wiped up the mess.

New believers faced constant pressure from their non-Christian neighbors to go back to the spirits, so we printed illustrated booklets we called *What Does a Christian Do?* He prays. He doesn't do demon worship or tie his wrists with string. He attends worship service. He thanks God for food. When he builds his new house or plants his rice field, he prays to God instead of doing demon worship. He sings hymns. He is baptized and takes communion.

When two new Christian young people wanted to get married, we saw it as a wonderful opportunity for us to demonstrate the Christian way to do things. The Pwo Karen way meant getting drunk.

Young people, we learned, were holding back in their commitment to Christ because they didn't know how to find a wife except in the old heathen way. At funerals young men and women march around the bier of the dead person for several days singing love songs to each other.

Parents who followed Karen customs arranged marriages for their children based on material gain or status. It is considered very good if a family without fields marries into a family with fields; and the family with fields is anxious to get another worker. For the Christian, mutual faith in Christ must be the first consideration. Yet how can a Christian get married if there are no Christians to marry? Marriage is a big hurdle for most tribal groups where a young church is emerging and old customs give way to new Christian patterns. We didn't want to impose our western customs on them. Instead, we wanted to preserve the good part of their traditions and replace demon customs with meaningful Christian ones.

When Nang Dee and Bite got married we worked out a pattern for a Christian marriage. Bonfires glowed in the dusk as Karen Christians gathered at Prosperity Fields, waiting expectantly for the first Christian wedding—a celebration that would last two nights. Many people had come from other villages to see how a Karen could get married without getting drunk enough to sing ribald songs all night. "How can it be fun without rice whiskey?" they wondered.

When a truck arrived loaded with people, we heard a shout, "He's coming!" It was the groom, a tall, good-looking young man, and his family and friends from a distant village. Wedding guests gathered at the church to receive the bridegroom. A big kettle of strong tea sweetened with condensed milk was offered in place of the customary whiskey. "Will they like it?" we wondered, or would they reject it as a weak substitute? Apparently it would do. They smiled and laughed as they passed around the glasses until they had drained three huge buckets of it.

The groom appeared, peering out from a towel draped around his shoulders. His best man was a shorter, clean-cut quiet man who had married Geekay's oldest daughter. Both men had only recently turned from demons to Christ and hadn't had much teaching yet.

After singing and prayers the two "go-betweens" made speeches, then everyone—young and old—played a game in which they matched cards. "It's that one. No, this one." Granny Scratch beat a cocky young man while we all watched, cheered and hollered. Late that night we fell asleep hearing Karen voices rising and falling in conversation, but that was far better than drunken singing.

At dawn the next morning, they slaughtered a huge pig which they had brought from a distant village. Marriage was a hot issue in that village, so three Christians came to see how this affair would be conducted. Several men made a fire outside and poured a bucket of water into two giant woks for the traditional wedding stew. They chopped pork on big trays and threw it into the boiling pot. They toasted and pounded rice grain into flour to thicken it. Women cut vegetables, added seasonings, and stoked the fires. One man whittled a long stick to stir the thick, bubbly mixture. Herbs gathered from the forest made it especially tasty. Each household brought a round black lacquered eating tray with mounds of cooked rice, and they ladled out bowls of steaming peppery stew. After grace, everyone feasted to his heart's content.

Next, the Christians gathered in the church for the ceremony. The bride appeared at last in her worn but clean long white tunic—the last time she'd ever wear the single girl's dress. Three years ago Nang Dee had been a tiny mousy girl, shy, awkward, pale, sickly and unattractive. Village people labeled her helpless and hopeless. Her father and several older brothers were either in jail or murdered for involvement in opium. Two older sisters had disgusted the village by becoming second wives of men already married.

When Nang Dee came to Christ, she emerged like a butterfly from her cocoon. Her appearance changed so much after taking worm medicine and vitamins that she now glowed with health and cleanliness. Mentally her mind awakened with the exercise of reading. Spiritually she became a sweet, faithful believer in the Lord, still shy, but firm in her faith. Her bridesmaid, Doo Boo, had graduated from grade school and was now working for us. In her white dress, she was a beautiful girl, inwardly and outwardly. The two girls stood out in shining contrast to the unbelieving girls, leading us to nod knowingly, "Yes, Christ makes a difference!"

Both bride and groom seemed very shy as they sat in the front of the group. With great embarrassment, and to everyone's amusement, they fed each other some chicken, rice and water. This was a traditional Karen wedding custom, and we couldn't discover any connection with spirits. It was simply a token of their commitment to care for each other. Afterwards the couple each placed a hand on God's Word while others offered prayers of blessing and a short exhortation about duties in a Christian marriage. Of course they made no offerings to spirits.

Now the bride returned with her friends to her house to sew up the seam of her new outfit. She put off the old white dress forever as she donned the new bright red embroidered tunic and red skirt she had woven herself and that married ladies wear. Again, this was an old custom, but had no connection to spirits.

After the evening feast, the couple met once more to kneel at the front of the church. The bride in her new red outfit brought the groom a bag, a blanket and a shirt she had woven by hand and which he immediately put on. Then she took the things out her bag and put them into his. As a sort of bride price the groom presented the bride's mother with a gift of some hoes. And after more exhortation and prayers, the crowd escorted them to her house where they sang some more. One by one everyone left, except for the immediate families.

Finally, the next morning, after another feast, families and friends piled into a pickup to escort the couple to the groom's village about 32 miles away. Nang Dee carried her belongings in a small basket on her back. It was hard for her to leave the Christian friends and the teaching she so loved, but she would find new Christian friends. Geekay's oldest daughter would be there and the two new Christian couples could learn together. Maybe she could even teach Geekay's daughter to read. She'd be living with her in-laws who were new Christians, although her new father-in-law was still on opium. Then there were her husband's two young sisters and a little brother. It would not be easy to live with the whole family sleeping around the same fire. Perhaps next year her husband would make her a new house.

As soon as she arrived in her husband's village Nang Dee picked up the water buckets and followed Geekay's daughter who showed her the way to the well. As the new wife she would be expected to work. This was more than just a marriage of two people. I thought of the Scripture which says that God has put us on display, and I realized that this was a public performance of great significance that would set a pattern for the whole Karen church.

Great questions still hung over this couple until their first child was born. Some watched to see if babies could be born in this new Christian way without whiskey or incantations to the spirits, without tying string on their wrists. And when it happened and a bouncing baby boy was born to the Christian couple, it opened the way for more teenagers to take an open stand for Christ.

Freedom from the old spirit customs helped the Karen in some very practical ways. Without the old taboos, they could learn new methods for making fields more productive. A Swiss OMF agriculturist came with a work party to demonstrate how crops could be improved and new crops grown by the modern method of strip farming. Mr. Dee agreed to use some of his fields for the demonstration.

Fifteen Swiss young people came to live in Prosperity Fields for a month where they worked in the hot sun along with the Karen people. Unable to speak the language, they showed by their hard work, clean lives and joyous faces that they were Christians. They brought tools and seeds, showed Mr. Dee how to use the new plow blade, and helped Beng Vang pull stumps.

Like all babies, new Christians are very dependent and the Karen were no exception. The Karen looked to us for help in every problem that came along, including sickness and earning a living. We couldn't be everywhere at the same time, of course, so we worked at weaning them from dependence on us and at teaching them to depend on God. There was so much to learn once they were free from the power of the demons, but when they believed the gospel and stepped out in faith, they saw God work. God helped Geekay find good fields. Another man discovered a way to irrigate his fields when the missionary's advice failed. U Vang trusted God to protect him as he worked fields that others were afraid to work because they were cursed. A few Christians were mature enough to help new believers burn their demon things and to call other believers together for worship. All of them needed to make the Word an increasing part of their daily diet and assimilate it into their living.

When we saw how much time it was taking to care for these young believers, we looked for ways to multiply ourselves. We had to find leaders to train who in turn could care for others. A few young people who could speak Thai went to the Bible school at Phayao. Others took a shorter training course at Maesariang.

There was no school, however, for those who spoke only Karen, so on one weekend a month we gathered Christian leaders together for intensive teaching. In spite of the obstacles, the new way was spreading outwardly in all directions, taking root inwardly, and the infants in Christ began slowly to grow.

# 15

## INFANT CHURCH IN SOP LAN
## 1975

We were just a few weeks away from leaving Striped Creek for furlough when Mr. Dee brought the message.

"Jot Saw orders you to come to his village."

Who in the world is Jot Saw? We had never heard of him, nor of his village, Sop Lan. At the field conference in February, we had reported that the Pwo Karen church had grown from to 245 believers by early 1977. Fifteen years after we had moved to our first home in Wangloong on the plain, God had begun to set the Pwo Karen free. He had shown in a marvelous way that he is stronger than the spirits. We were half-packed for home, already feeling the pangs of leaving this tender young church. But, we knew there were capable younger missionaries on hand, and, ultimately, it belonged to the Lord. Before we left, however, it seemed that God had one more thing to teach us.

Sop Lan is about 45 miles from Striped Creek over some very difficult terrain. Besides it's in Sgaw Karen territory, and Jim argued with Mr. Dee. "I don't speak Sgaw."

"But his wife is Pwo and speaks our dialect. He'll understand you," Mr. Dee insisted. "He's a very influential man. If he orders, you must go. And, besides, some of the villagers are Pwo Karen, and the rest will understand you."

So with Mr. Dee and several others, Jim started off down the narrow mining road in the Land-Rover. Rain had washed deep ruts in the trail and had eaten away the steep dirt banks. The road hadn't been used for a long time, and it was overgrown with brush and bamboo. At one point the Land-Rover churned up a steep hill, but just before the top the wheels spun and the vehicle began to slide back. A branch caught the door and ripped it off, but Jim was able to stop. The men got out, cut bamboo branches, and laid them in the ruts. Once more the Land-Rover lurched forward and this time inched its way over the top. From there on the road serpentined up and down the mountains until the village came in sight.

Headman Jot Saw welcomed the weary travelers up to his porch. His wife set a pot of rice on the fire and began cooking a meal. While she did that Jim took out his cassette recorder and began playing a tape of the gospel message in Pwo Karen. Suddenly Jot Saw jumped up.

"That's it," he shouted. "Those are the words—Jesus is stronger than the spirits." He began calling his friends to hear, and the story poured out.

It had happened while we were still living in Wangloong. One day Jot Saw had been sitting on his porch and noticed an old tribal man emerging from the jungle. For a moment the man stopped, unwound the red turban from his head and wiped the sweat from his face. Rewinding his turban, he bent over his load and trod slowly down the village path.

Jot Saw noticed that something in the old man's red shoulder bag weighed him down, so he asked, "What do you have there, Uncle Bee?"

"A box that talks our own Karen language. Want to hear it?"

Jot Saw was skeptical but intrigued. "Sure! How can a box talk?"

Uncle Bee climbed the ladder to Jot Saw's porch, took a slim green box out of his bag, inserted a handle, and cranked it.

Then he put a round black plate on the box, adjusted the needle, placed it on the plate, and it spun round and round. Suddenly, just as the old man said, the box began to talk words that Jot Saw could understand. Now fascinated, he stared at the box as it talked about God creating the world and the Karen people.

Jot Saw remembered that his grandfather had told him that God created people in the beginning of the world. It was an old Karen legend, but the legends also said that God went away and left the Karen. And since that time Karen have sacrificed pigs and chickens to the spirits instead of worshiping their Creator. But the voice in the box added something new to the story. God didn't leave them, the voice insisted. God loved the Karen and is more powerful than the spirits. The box even sang, "Jesus Loves Me, This I Know." This was big news and Jot Saw questioned the old man.

"Where did you get this box, Uncle Bee?"

"When I went down to Wangloong market to buy salt," he told Jot Saw. "I saw a bunch of Karen standing around the doorway of a house. I went closer and saw a white man playing this box with the Karen words. I wanted to listen over and over again, so finally I bought the box from the man, and he gave me these two records with it."

"Uncle Bee, would you like to sell that box to me?" Jot Saw asked cautiously, and the negotiation began.

"Well, I see you are very keen to have it! How much will you give me?"

"One hundred baht."

"Oh, come now! I'll take no less than 500 baht."

Back and forth they went until Headman Jot Saw waggled Uncle Bee down to 400 baht and the talking box became his.

Day and night the Jot Saw listened to the box until he had memorized both sides of the two black records. The words rang in his mind: "Jesus is greater than the spirits." That meant he was greater than the rice spirit, the water spirit, the spirits of the dead, the ancestor spirits. How could that be?

All his life Jot Saw had been afraid of the spirits. If he misbehaved his mother had threatened that the spirits would bite him and make him sick. Once he had a raging fever and went to see a demon priest. The priest reached into his bag, pulled out some chicken bones, studied them, the looked at Jot Saw. "You have committed a grave sin," he told the headman. "Two days ago when you went to your field, you did not return by the same path. Your spirits couldn't find their way back home, so now they're causing your fever. You must sacrifice a white chicken and a black chicken to call the spirits back home. Then you must tie them in with strings around your wrists."

Jot Saw didn't want to kill his chickens, but he wanted to get well. So he did what the priest said to do, and he got well. The spirits are very powerful. So the message from the box was exciting news. After several years, however, the box no longer spoke, so Jot Saw wrapped it in an old bag and set it back on the shelf.

Meanwhile, Jot Saw grew rich and powerful. He owned several elephants and hired them out to work in the logging business. While others slashed and burned down the jungle to make new fields on the hillside, Jot Saw cut down trees on level ground for his rice paddies. He dug a ditch to channel in water and built a small dike to hold it in. He planted rice seeds in one corner and watched the lime green seedlings come up thick and rich. When the rains came, he plowed the fields with his buffalo and everyone in his village helped him transplant the seedlings in straight rows in the soggy fields. He weeded them and watched the stalks tassel into grain. When they turned yellow and the heavy ripe grain heads dropped, he cut the stalks with a curved sickle and bound them into sheaves. Then he dried them, placed the sheaves on a mat, and beat the grains off the stalks with a large wooden paddle. He harvested more grain than he could use for his family, so he hired poor families to help and paid them rice for wages. He was a very rich and clever man.

For all his wealth and cleverness, however, Jot Saw struggled with a big opium habit. At first it had seemed relaxing to lay by the fire and puff his pipe and dream. But then he needed more and more opium, and it became a very expensive habit. He could see his lush fields and pigs and elephants being sucked down the opium pipe. He knew other rich men who had been ruined by the habit.

When he learned about a medicine man who claimed he could break people from opium, Jot Saw sent for him. For several days the medicine man stuck by him. Sometimes he prayed or rubbed Jot Saw's legs or, when the pain became unbearable, pushed him into the cold stream. Sometimes he laid a black Bible on Jot Saw's chest and chanted some words. The medicine man was from Burma and said he was a Christian, but he couldn't read the Bible. Instead he used it like a charm. "It has Jesus power," he explained.

"Jesus power!" Jot Saw remembered the record player and knew he had to find out more about this Jesus. He recovered from his opium habit, but knew that if he was going to stay off of it, he needed Jesus.

One day a neighbor said to him, "You know, my wife's relatives up north no longer worship the spirits. They now worship Jesus. The white missionary teaches them."

That's when Jot Saw sent for Jim. The relative he spoke of was Mrs. Dee Waters in Prosperity Fields.

When Jim heard the story, he marveled. It was another display of God's power and perfect timing. Jim and Jot Saw sat up late that night while Jim taught him more about Jesus—how He loves and cares for people, how He has power to calm the storm, make the blind see and the crippled walk. In spite of this, he explained, wicked men killed Him by nailing Him to a cross. And after He was dead, He proved He had power even over death, and He became alive.

The next morning Jot Saw announced, "I'm ready to believe." With Jot Saw's knife, Jim cut the strings off his wrists. Then he stirred the fire, gathered up the feathers and strings and bamboo sticks that festooned the doorway and burned them all.

"Now," Jim explained, "we'll pray, and you must repeat the words after me. 'Oh God, who created heaven and earth. We thank you that you are stronger than the spirits. Thank you for sending your Son, Jesus, to deliver us from the evil spirits. Thank you that you defeated Satan and all his helpers on the cross. Please forgive our sins and send your Holy Spirit to dwell in our hearts and protect us from the evil spirits forever. Amen!'"

Jot Saw beamed. "Now you go to my neighbors house."

"Okay," Jim agreed, "but you have to come with me. I'll have to leave you soon, but Jesus will be here. He'll never leave you. You must carry on the work and help others turn to God."

Together the two men went to the next two houses. Jot Saw watched carefully as Jim went through the ceremony again. In the next five houses, Jot Saw cut off the demon strings, burned the fetishes, and led the family in prayer. This brand new Christian, for all practical purposes, was now their pastor.

Before Jim left, Jot Saw gathered all the families on his porch and Jim taught them to pray and gave them some very basic instructions in the faith.

"Every Sunday you must gather here, listen to the cassette player, sing the songs and pray. Whatever happens, don't do demon worship. Instead, pray to Jesus—about everything."

With deep reluctance and a lot of questions, Jim made the trek back to Striped Creek. These baby believers seemed like flickering lights in an immense sea of darkness. How could they hold onto their new faith without a teacher? How would they stand up to the taunts of neighbors? What would they do the first time someone got sick? Would they keep on course for the long months ahead? It was a long trip home and Jim had a lot of time to pray.

# 16

## PASSING IT ON
## 1976-1977

When we returned to Thailand a year later, we set out as soon as we could for Sop Lan village, not knowing what to expect. We believed God was able to keep those believers, but, after all, they had had less than a day's worth of discipling.

For one thing, we learned quickly that the road hadn't improved. It was so overgrown that at times the bamboo closed in over our heads. Suddenly we came to a cluster of huts which Jim distinctly remembered had not been there the year before. A Karen lady carrying buckets of water on a pole set down her load and looked at us. And as we got out of the Land-Rover she exclaimed, "Jo Dee, you've come back!"

We were startled. How did these people know us? Jim was sure she wasn't among the group he met before.

"You must come and talk to Brother Two," she insisted, and led us to a hut where a man sat with his wife who was nursing a baby.

"We've been waiting for you to come," Brother Two announced. "We lived in another village, but we all became sick. We sacrificed many pigs, but still people died. The demons don't help us. We heard that people in Sop Lan don't

140

worship demons anymore. Now they worship Jesus. We didn't know when you'd come back, so we moved our houses out here to the main road, so that when you came back, you would stop and tell us how we can turn to Jesus." We sat hardly believing what we heard. The desperation in his tone moved us deeply. Eagerly Jim explained the gospel to them and at their request removed their demon strings and burned them.

Going on toward Sop Lan our Land-Rover got stuck in the mud crossing a creek. But the Sop Lan villagers heard the motor and ran out to help us out and to welcome us. Again to our amazement, we found that God had been working. Jot Saw and five of the families were faithfully coming to Jot Saw's house every Sunday to listen to the cassette player and to sing and pray. When Karen from other villages visited Sop Lan, they noticed the fat healthy pigs and the numerous chickens which had time to grow because they weren't used for sacrifices. It was visible evidence that Jesus was stronger than the demons.

Meanwhile, Jot Saw had dramatically demonstrated his faith in an encounter with his friend, Che Louie. At that time few wild elephants still roamed the mountains of Thailand. Most of them had been captured and trained to work. Huge as they are elephants are sure-footed and push through the jungle where there are no roads. Loggers taught the beasts to roll logs with their broad foreheads and prod them with their tusks. With a log chained to a harness, an elephant can drag it through the forest and out to the highway where a truck can haul it away.

Jot Saw owned several elephants which he used for hauling teak logs. One day he and Che Louie from Long Village were working together. Each man had a heavy teak log hooked on to his elephant, and each sat on top of his elephant's massive head, using a hook to tap the beast to go left or right. Part way up a steep hill about a mile from the village, the elephant began to strain, so Jot Saw shouted, "Go! Go!" and kicked the animal behind his big flapping ears.

141

Che Louie had the same problem. His elephant was bigger, but the hill was steep and the animal refused to go any further. Che Louie prodded with his hook, but it only enraged the elephant which let out a loud bellow. The two men beat the animals, kicked them and shouted at them, but they wouldn't budge. They just lifted their trunks and roared.

Che Louie slipped off his elephant and told Jot Saw, "I guess we'll have to do some demon worship. Perhaps that will give the elephants some strength. We just can't leave these valuable logs here in the jungle." So he pulled some feathers and bones out of a bag and began chanting prayers to the spirits.

Jot Saw got off his elephant, too, and as he did, he remembered what the teacher, Jo Dee, had told him. "When you have a problem, don't do demon worship. Instead, pray to Jesus. He'll help you." So he explained to Che Louie, "I don't worship demons anymore. I've entered Jesus, and my teacher told me that Jesus is stronger than the demons."

"How stupid!" Louie laughed. "Do you believe all that foreign stuff? How can Jesus hear you? I can't see him." And he went on doing his demon worship.

Meanwhile, Jot Saw knelt on the ground, folded his hands and prayed, "Strong Jesus, you can see we can't get these logs up the hill. I'm not going to worship demons anymore, so I ask you to help me. Give my elephant strength to pull this log up the hill."

With that he scrambled back onto the elephant and firmly nudged his foot behind a big ear. The elephant strained, leaned forward, and slowly began to pull the heavy load forward over the crest of the hill.

Che Louie stared with open mouth. "If he can do it, I can too," he thought. My elephant's bigger. So he climbed back up and began shouting and kicking. The elephant strained, leaned forward, and Che Louie shouted and kicked harder. But that's as far as the animal went. The elephant and rider remained in the same place. Disgusted and bewildered Che Louie unhooked his elephant, rode back to the village without his log, and confronted his friend.

"Brother, I want that Jesus power," he told Jot Saw. "He is stronger than the demons. Tell me more about him."

So Jot Saw got out the gospel record player and let Che Louie hear the message. And after many hours he went back to his village to tell his family and friends.

Now it was Che Louie's turn to change. He had smoked opium, but he made up his mind to break the habit. He took his shotgun, sat on the porch, and announced, "If anyone comes near me with opium, I'll shoot him." Day after day he took this stance until finally the terrible craving left him.

When Jim and I returned from furlough, we heard that Che Louie had been to Striped Creek three times looking for us. He was a tall man with a wise face, and he urged us to come to his village. "If you can't walk, I'll send my elephant to carry you," he promised.

"No thanks," Jim smiled, thinking that he would get seasick riding on that beast over the narrow, steep trails. "I'd rather walk."

It took Jim eight hours to trek the hills to Long Village, but the people there listened carefully to every word. It was all new to them. The little bit Che Louie had told them had created a thirst to know more. Immediately several families cut off their demon strings and burned them. Then they butchered a goat to celebrate the occasion. Only one thing dampened it for Jim. As he watched, they emptied the goat's gall bladder into the bubbling stew. "That's to give it flavor," they explained.

Che Louie had his own graphic way of teaching. "When I worshiped evil spirits, every good thing went out from my heart, down my arms and hands and dropped out through my fingers. My pigs, chickens, rice and money all disappeared to keep the spirits happy. Now that I believe God it all comes back to me." He drew his left hand over his right arm up to his heart. "My pigs grow fat; my chickens get big enough to lay eggs and hatch more chickens. Christ gives me so much. He

143

fills my heart with great joy."

It may sound a little like a health and wealth gospel to western ears, but pigs, chickens and rice are vital for the Karen. They're not an extra. Che Louie was saying that the true God had, along with the gift of eternal life, given him more rice and animals. The good news must start where the Karen feel their deep needs.

We also learned that Che Louie had a gift for teaching in parables, even though he couldn't read the Bible. "People who worship evil spirits instead of Jesus," he taught, "are like a man walking along a hot dusty trail. The man comes to a spring of fresh water and washes his hands and arms and face but doesn't take a drink to quench his thirst. For a short time he feels refreshed, but as he walks on, he soon feels thirsty and faint again because he failed to drink of the water when he had the opportunity."

The gospel, to our deep satisfaction, was spreading. And God was doing it in such a way that we had to point to His hand in it. In remote places we had never heard of, and could hardly get to, one Karen told another and people turned to Christ. He was fulfilling the promise that He would build His church. He was beginning something that the gates of hell could not prevail against. And now He was doing it with Karen materials and Karen leadership. He will deliver the captives from the Strong Man as he had promised. He will save our children.

# PART III
# A NEW GENERATION
## 1994

*Christmas celebration, 1994*

# 17
## THE RETURN
## 1994

The little package arrived at our apartment in Singapore one morning in November. I noticed that the postage was from Thailand, but that wasn't unusual. We often received mail from there. We had been working at OMF International headquarters for about four years, but we still had strong ties to the North Thailand field. It was a cassette, not a letter, however, so I waited until Jim came home for lunch and we switched on the cassette player.

Karen voices began to sing, and then a familiar voice began to speak.

"Jo Dee, our hearts long for you. It's been a long time since you visited us. Can you come to join us for Christmas this year? We want to hear you teaching us. We are lonesome to hear your voice. Please come!"

We looked at each other silently, knowing the other's thoughts. We missed them, too. Part of our hearts was in those mountains. How good it would be to celebrate Christmas with Pwo Karen believers. "Lord, would it be possible? It would be so wonderful."

We could picture them hovering over the recorder making this tape. It took a lot of work on their part. Probably the resident missionary gave them our address, but inviting us to join them for Christmas in Striped Creek was obviously their own idea.

So it was that fourteen years after we moved away from Striped Creek, we found ourselves driving down the road from Chiangmai to Hod in the old white Toyota four-door pickup Jim had used when he was Field Leader of North Thailand.

So much had changed in that time. The highway was now wider and paved. Big new factories had sprung up from the rice paddies. Thriving agricultural developments lined both sides of the road. An irrigation project had turned dry, barren land into gardens and fields and wild land had become fruit orchards. We passed the Canaan project where Mrs. Glass once lived. She was gone now, on to her heavenly reward, but the Thai church was thriving and the leprosy project has a prosperous honey business and mango orchard.

We stopped to see Boy Jee, his wife and family, still living near Sandy Creek and still, faithful to the Lord. Their brown wrinkled faces broke into beaming smiles as they embraced us and told us how they still trusted the Lord and would never go back to the demons. One son, an opium addict, had died, but other children and grandchildren continued to follow God in spite of the little teaching they received. Whenever they could they attended the Thai church.

Hod had become a bustling crossroads, and over a lunch of coke and fried rice, we noticed Karen people with their distinctive red costumes mingling in the new marketplace. So much more was available in the new shops but the prices were higher, too. A new hospital and a medicine shop had opened since we were there last.

In early days it took a day and a half to walk from Wangloong, just down the road from Hod, up the mountain to Striped Creek. In the truck it took us just two hours. And that's where we got the big shock. We saw a telephone booth in NaFawn village and a store stood at the entrance of Striped Creek village. Poles with electric wires lined the road, and we imagined such things as electric lights, fans, refrigerators. etc. And TV would surely introduce the outside world to this village that once seemed like the end of the world. It was, of course, inevitable. A mining company had come in and was providing jobs. A Thai army doctor had set up his practice near the new school. Huge tomato and cabbage gardens flanked the road providing both income and better nutrition. The outside world improved the quality of living and increased the quantity of enticements.

On the hill overlooking the village loomed a large Buddhist temple. We had come to the mountains hoping to introduce Christ to the Karen before Buddhism made inroads into their lives. Now here it was, staring us in the face. The village headman who had once been cured of a skin disease by missionary medicine, developed an ear for the Thai government officials who brought in a school. Along with that came the temple and Thai school teachers who introduced gambling and drinking. They sent some of the students, including Geekay's nephew, a bright little boy, to train as Buddhist novices.

And there stood our wooden house with its big veranda jutting out over the driveway and the deep red bougainvillaea cascading over the fence. Karen children heard our pickup coming and ran up to the porch steps to greet us. "Jo Dee, Granny White, you've come back!" We lit a fire in the fire box, dug our blankets out of the barrels and slipped back very quickly into the familiar role. Soon people came with their sick, wanting medicines, telling us about their aches and pains, physical and spiritual.

It was good to be back. We could hardly wait for the celebration. This year the church at Striped Creek was hosting the Christmas celebration for other Pwo Karen villages. The men were busy building a platform that extended the weathered bamboo church building. They stopped to greet us with huge smiles on faces dripping with sweat—Tu, the youngest son of Headman Note, Jo Po, his sister's husband, Mang Jo, our next door neighbor, and Mang Bite, his brother. Young people carried in fragrant green pine boughs and began decorating the church with streamers of colored paper, strings of balloons and bright greeting cards sent from abroad. Some people raked leaves and cleaned up the grounds. Women pounded rice in preparation for the coming feast.

That evening after supper we sat on mats around the front room fire talking with visitors. Their warm hearts matched the fire, enchanting us once again with the joy of having these people as our friends. Now they were part of our family in Christ. They asked about our work and our family and our children. Many of them had faded photos of our family stuck on their wall. "We pray every day for you and your children," they told us.

When they left, holding burning torches to light their way home, we stood on the porch and gazed into the cold crisp night. Stars in the black sky above shone so much more brightly than in the city. Looking up we searched for the three bright stars of Orion's belt. They were still there and they had not changed. We almost felt we could see the Christmas Star.

The next morning began before daylight with the sputter and put-putting of the electric rice mill which had replaced the steady thump-thump of the old wooden rice pounders. A motorcycle roared off to work, and a pickup drove in to collect day laborers. We set out to renew acquaintances. As they greeted us and looked into our faces, our minds reeled trying to remember their names and recognize the younger ones who were now several years older. With customary candor they exclaimed, "Jo Dee, you are just the same as before! Granny White, you are fatter! And you have more grey hair!"

It was odd to sit back and watch the Karen Christians do the planning and preparing to host about 300 guests for overnight and three meals. Years ago we bought the meat, cooked the meal, planned the program, decorated the church and transported everyone. But then we had a much smaller crowd.

A pickup drove up, and the dusty figures of Boon Ruang and Muti stepped out and vigorously greeted us. Both had married local girls and become active leaders at Sop Lan. Boon Ruang was the pastor of the church and Muti, the headman of the village. Sadly we learned that Headman Jot Saw had been viciously murdered. His death stirred up many questions. "Doesn't God protect His people? If God delivers from the power of demons why doesn't He deliver from the power of bad men? Aren't Christians impervious to bullets? Who would take his place as leader?" The church continued strong, however, spreading to more than thirty satellite villages.

At some point we realized that it was the second generation, sons and daughters of those who became believers when we were there, who were now leading the celebration. They were the ones who stood in our doorway and watched what we did all day long.

The slightly bent figure of Mrs. Dee Waters, with a new pink satin turban wrapped around her head and pounds of beads draped like a rainbow around her neck, climbed onto our porch and took our hands in hers, her small face beaming. She had survived many disappointments since she first believed.

We recalled that awful day when Mrs. Waters tried to commit suicide because her husband took a second wife. Jim had walked down to his field house to talk to him. "For five years you have been my right hand man," he told him. "You learned to read God's Word and were leading the church here. Why have you given all that up now to take this woman?"

"How do I know if God is real or not?" he told Jim. "I can look at a pair of trousers and tell you if they're good or not. But I can't see Jesus. Besides, Abraham and other men in the Bible took two wives. What's so bad about that?"

About that same time Doo Boo, Mrs. Dee's beautiful petite daughter, who had graduated from Bible school, made a disappointing choice. She turned down the offer of a fine Christian man from Pine Village, and decided to marry the headman's son—a dashing, clever Karen man who got a Thai education and became a school teacher, but not a Christian.

When Mr. Dee and his daughter both took these backward

step the baby church in Prosperity nearly fell apart. They had been the leaders and no one else was able to preach or teach Sunday school. Their fall had an effect on other believers who looked to them for leadership. In Pine village, Beng Vang's oldest son, Jo Gate, turned back and worshiped demons again. Christians in Pine all turned back except for the young man, Bee Thout, whom Doo Boo had turned down.

Mr. Dee hadn't come for today's Christmas celebration, but Doo Boo, still beautiful, shy and smiling, came with her mother. She had faithfully carried on after missionaries left, teaching Sunday school and keeping the church going through its ups and downs, but her husband had never believed.

Mrs. Dee stood proudly for a photo with her three oldest children, Doo Boo, Jody and Jobe who had followed the Lord, taken Bible training and were now experienced leaders in the Karen church. Excitedly, they told us about other members of the family who had turned to Christ, too. Even old Grandpa Waters who had held out for so many years, turned to God in his last days.

Quiet, gentle Jody was busy setting up the public address system he had borrowed from the Omkoy hospital where his wife worked. "Testing ... one, two, three." He knew exactly how to run the system and soon had the church completely wired for sound and light and the public address system working so all could hear. Jody had married a tribal girl and studied at Phayao Bible School where he faced a difficult choice. He had to write a paper for a class, so he had asked Jim for information about the Pwo people. As he read how God had worked among his own people, his heart was stirred to return. So he and his wife moved to Omkoy to help the Karen church there. He also taught Christian education in the Thai school. Now he was the elected president of the Pwo Karen churches.

We never thought Jody's brother, Jobe, would be able to study because he had weak eyes. But he got glasses and he too went to Phayao. And now he was back helping his home church in Prosperity Fields.

The sun was beginning its golden descent behind the mountains as we walked towards the decorated church. People stood in clumps in front of the church chatting as they waited for the service to begin. Jody was already playing the music tapes to gather people, and Jobe, in purple warmups, and Tu with his big smile and guitar, were calling the people to come to worship.

Mrs. Note, the former headman's wife, threaded her way through the crowd, grabbed our hands and gazed up into our eyes. "We're so glad to see you." Her husband had been murdered on their front porch. He never turned to Christ, and his sudden death shattered the whole family, suddenly demoting them from their leadership position and filling them with fear of those who had killed their husband and father. But in their distress Mrs. Note and most of her children—two daughters, Bite and Mung, and their husbands, and her two sons, Dee Keng and Tu, and their wives—turned to the Lord. God had softened her heart and lips, and was now using her bright, gifted children to help the Pwo church to grow.

Tu was now in his second year of Bible school at Phayao. As a five-year-old he had been sitting beside his headman father on the porch when bandits walked up and shot his father in the face. The memory never faded, but now his mind was filled with God's word and ways. His small stature and natural leadership abilities reminded us of his father, and his gift of gab and big smile were now helpful gifts in the church.

He stood up front smiling broadly, "So glad all you folks have come! You've come from many places. Let's see how many from Grass? Raise your hands! How many from Omkoy? From Sop Lan? How many walked all the way from Long Village? From Mae Tom? From Dusty? From Pine? From Striped Creek? How many are here for the first time—for your first Christmas? Thank God for all of you! Now, you Christians from Striped Creek, invite these folks into your homes for the night and make them feel welcome!" Tu's enthusiasm infected the people, and they responded with warm smiles and friendly banter.

Everyone clapped for several families from Latta Key, a village on the other side of the road. They had recently turned to the Lord, and Tu was teaching them how to read and preparing them for baptism. They planned to build a church soon in their village.

Dee Keng and a Canadian missionary, Nancy Stephens, had prepared a new edition of the hymnbook and almost completed the Pwo New Testament. What they had finished up to Hebrews was printed and published in a neat little black New Testament which we brought with us. We hauled the cardboard box out of the truck and opened it.

"Our own Bible! It looks like the Thai Bible! In our own language!" Karen young people opened the black covers and smoothed the fine pages of India paper with their rough hands as they began to read.

Eighteen years ago when his father was murdered, Dee had fled the village and stayed away for several years. It had been a great day when he came back. The translation work had been weighing heavily on Jim's heart, and he needed an educated Pwo Christian to help. Dee fit the task wonderfully.

Now here on the stage Nang Mung, Dee Keng's sister, was taking charge of her little Sunday school group of children who came up front to perform a nativity drama. Mary and Joseph in robes shyly took their places beside the little basket of hay in the center. Angels in white dresses and gold paper headbands fluttered in and performed a dance of praise. Bright-eyed shepherds with shrouded heads and wooden staffs filed in followed by little "sheep" crawling on all fours under cotton blankets. Dignified wise men robed in thick towels and towering crowns presented their shiny gifts.

When Nang Mung was a little girl there was no Sunday school. As she grew older she developed a burden for children and pleaded to start a Sunday school to teach them. But Nang Mung and her husband, Jo Po, had a stormy marriage. Everyone knew about their big fights and knew that Jo Po had been unfaithful to her. She had been at the point of throwing him out, but he repented and she took him back. Both of them attended the training school in Maesariang. Now he had built her a nice house and they were doing better.

More skits followed the Christmas story. One skit featured a seeker asking questions such as:

"Can I believe in Jesus and still make merit at the temple?"

"If I turn to Jesus what will happen to my unbelieving relatives? Will the demons bite them and take revenge on them?"

"If I'm a Christian can I still dress like a Karen person?"

"Will God make me sick if I don't go to church every Sunday?"

These were very real problems for many young believers, and here we had mature Karen Christians (not white missionaries providing answers), helping their brothers and sisters grow in the faith.

Jim rose to speak, and all eyes fastened on him. Would he remember the language after being away so long? He wondered himself if he'd have the freedom he'd had before. But as he began to speak the words came back, and he told the wonderful story of how God loved the Karen people and had power to deliver them from demons and sin and of how Jesus, by His death on the cross, provided a way back to a right relationship with God.

Next Jody and Jobe, adjusted the screens and loud speakers and started a film. Many other villagers pressed into the crowd, wanting to hear, but hoping the darkness would hide their identity from the Christians. Not everyone understood the Thai sound track, but at the end Tu tried to summarize the story in Karen language. When Jim showed slides of the people themselves, they laughed and pointed at each other. "That's you, Bee! And that's Mrs. Note—she has on her old hat. There's Bite. What's he doing? Carrying his hoe? Ha! Ha!"

Young people passed around trays of Karen sweets—glutinous rice pounded into a sticky mass with brown sugar and sesame seeds, and cone-shaped pockets made of banana leaves with steamed rice mixed with beans or peanuts inside. Finally, late in the evening the Striped Creek Christians took the visitors into their homes for the night.

A dozen crowing roosters heralded Christmas morning, and the pig penned up for the Christmas feast squealed in protest as it was taken to slaughter. Smoke curled from the open fires in front of the church where Jo Blay had started cooking the feast. Young girls clanked their buckets as they hurried to draw water from the well to fill the barrels. And while the preparations for the feast went on, Christians gathered in the church for an early morning prayer meeting.

Dee Keng stood up and read John 15 from the new Bible. With ease and poise he spoke on abiding in Christ and our need to have Christ's life within us to produce the good fruits of love, joy and peace. Then, taking his guitar, he taught the folks a new song he had composed and written.

Blind Joe and Mang Jo sat cross-legged on the bamboo floor. Years before when all the Christians had turned back to join the temple, Blind Joe had more spiritual sight than natural sight. In his travels to distant Karen villages looking for artifacts, he had met Sgaw Karen who believed in Jesus and sang gospel songs. "That's the truth! Why don't people in our village believe?" he wondered. He came to tell us he wanted to believe, along with Mang Jo who had been our next door neighbor for years, and Mang Jo's son, Jo Blay. These three ordinary families were the new shoots that appeared when it seemed that Satan and his hordes had snuffed out the church's flickering flame. From that small beginning now appeared all that we were seeing these days. Blind Joe and Mang Jo had their failures, too, but they still counted themselves Christians.

A few whacks on the gong announced breakfast. Jo Blay in a navy blazer and rubber thongs took charge of cooking the food. Young, shy and hard-working, Jo Blay and his bright-eyed wife, Dite, were children when we first moved to Striped Creek. Now he planned the meals, shopped for supplies, organized the cutting of the meat and vegetables, and stirred the huge cooking pots with a wooden paddle. As a young boy Jo Blay wanted to learn to read, but the village elders put a stop to that. He never learned to read fluently, but he always loved to sing the hymns. When he and Dite were first married it seemed they couldn't have children, but when they turned to God and prayed, God had answered. Now they had two little boys.

A line of people each bearing on their heads a black lacquered food tray with a mound of cooked rice on it began filing into the church. They shuffled around until they found a space on the floor to set down their tray and gather their family around. Extra people filled in gaps in the circles. A food crew moved through the clusters of people scooping hot steaming stew into an enamel bowl for each tray. Another whack on the gong brought a moment of quiet while one of the church leaders prayed. Then everyone dug in with their fingers.

All the reunions weren't so happy. We saw Geekay and his wife mingling in the crowd and remembered the sad day he decided he could make more money selling opium than working for us. We weren't surprised. We had noticed that his heart hadn't been into helping us the way it was at first. We felt badly for him and his family. We had invested so much time in teaching them, and they had helped us. But they had turned away, and now they seemed ill at ease among the believers.

A Karen lady brought a bouquet of red poinsettia flowers crammed into a glass jar, and placed them beside the offering bag on the pulpit at the front of the church. It was time for the morning service to begin.

Jo Po and Dee Keng strummed their guitars while Beng Vang's eldest and youngest daughters, from Dusty, led us in some action songs. We used the newly printed song books. Bong Jang stood up with his beaming smile and asked prayer for the group he heads in Grass Village. Tall, dark Bee Thout, leader at Pine Village, spoke quietly of hanging on to God even when others had turned back. Across the road we could hear the children singing in Nang Mung's Sunday school.

Finding it uncomfortable to sit so long on the concrete floor with my legs folded under me, I shifted my position. Jim rose to give the main message. What a thrill to hear the rustle of leaves as Karen believers turned their new Bibles to the scripture passage.

Another communal meal in the church followed the service.

Finally, inevitably, the time came to leave. We packed the pickup, and a few folks crawled in the back, hoping to catch a free ride to town. Others pressed on us tokens of their love and appreciation—a dusty plastic bag with rice, a big yellow pumpkin, a red shoulder bag they had woven and embroidered by hand.

"Are you going?" Their question began the customary way of saying goodbye.

"Yes, we're going. We'll pray for you very much."

"And we will pray for you. Our hearts will long for you."

Then the inevitable question: "When will you come back?"

"Not for a long time, but as soon as we can."

"Bye, bye," mothers lifted their babies' hands to wave.

We drove slowly down the driveway, past the children running and shouting, farther away from friends standing in front of our porch waving.

"It's so difficult to leave them. What will they do?"

"They'll be fine. They belong to the Lord. Look how he's taken care of them. How do you feel?"

"Like there is so much yet to be done. I wish I had ten lifetimes to spend here."

Our pickup paused to let some cows saunter across the highway and then moved on down the mountain into a different world.

# EPILOGUE

*Two years later,* at Easter, we made a brief trip back to the mountains and found the church building in Striped Creek rebuilt with concrete blocks and tile roofing. The spiritual church was also stronger, growing in numbers and knowledge of God, with the help of Rein and Maaike de Bel, an OMF couple from Holland.

One day we were introducing some new workers to the Karen Christians when they said to us, "Yes, Jo Dee, we're happy to have these people if you recommend them. But can't your son Nathan come back? We know him and we know his parents."

It was just a wish on a man's lips at the time. About a year later Nathan brought his wife and three little boys to see the village where he grew up. During that brief time God spoke to him.

"Dad," he said later. "I felt I couldn't do what you did. But when I visited this time I saw how much the infant Karen church needs teaching. Maybe—just maybe—we can help with that."

As I write Nathan and Kelly and their four boys have been accepted with OMF, and, if God so favors, they will some day take up the work of the gospel among the Pwo Karen in North Thailand, where Jim and I left off.

But more helpers are needed to go, give and pray so that this fledgling church will become established in God's Word Will you pray with us for others to join Nathan and Kelly as they go? Is God calling you ...


*For information on how you can be involved, contact*
**www.omf.org**

# CHARACTERS IN THE STORY—PWO KAREN PEOPLE

*Pwo Karen names are unusual for outsiders,*
*so we've provided a guide to the main characters in the book*

**Abel & Louie,** young Karen men from Hill Village on the plains; they helped us learn the language

**Bee Thout,** Karen leader in Pine Village

**Blind Joe,** one of the first believers in Striped Creek

**Bong Jang,** Karen leader in Grass Village

**Boon Ruang** from Burma, Bible School graduate who became national pastor in Sop Lan Village

**Bouy Dee,** Karen woman from Striped Creek with eclampsia

**Boy Jee and wife,** first believers in Sandy Creek on the plains, daughters: Date Mung, Gleck, Bee.

**Che Louie,** leader from Long village who owned elephants

**Chite Khwae,** man from Striped Creek who had an infected leg

**Dee Keng** in Striped Creek, son of Headman Note and helper in translation project

**Doo Boo** in Prosperity Fields, daughter of Mrs. Dee, Bible School graduate, married an unbeliever

**Geekay,** neighbor in Striped Creek, helper in language study and translation

**Headman Beng Vang** of Floating Fields Village; later moved to Dusty Village

**Headman Note** of Striped Creek, father of Dee Keng and Tu

**Headman Saturday** of Sandy Creek, succeeded Headman Spider and let us live in the village

**Headman Spider** first headman in Sandy Creek Village on the plains

**Headman Waters** of Prosperity Fields; called Grandpa Waters, father of Mr. Dee, grandfather of Jody

**Jo Blay,** Mang Jo's son, early believer in Striped Creek, married to Dite

**Jo Po,** Nang Mung's husband, Christian brother in law to Dee Keng and Tu

**Jobe,** son of Mr. and Mrs. Dee Waters, leader in Prosperity Fields church

**Jody,** son of Mr. and Mrs. Dee Waters whose crippled leg was corrected by surgery

**Joe Gate,** Beng Vang's son, lived in Pine Village, turned back

**Jot Saw,** Headman of Sop Lan, one of first believers, owned elephants

**Lohng Gahng,** woman from Splashing Creek with ovarian tumor

**Louie Paw,** Dee Bet's son, established a Christian center in Hope village

**Mang Jo,** Jo Blay's father, early believer in Striped Creek

**Mr. and Mrs. Gawk,** early believers from Sandy Creek on the plains

**Mrs. Glass and Uncle Silver and wife,** first Karen believers in Canaan, a rehabilitation village

**Mr. Dee Waters,** son of Headman Water's, father of Jody, Doo Boo and Jobe, took a second wife

**Mrs. Bite,** first demon priestess in Prosperity Fields, who turned to Christ and whose daughter died

**Mrs. Dee Waters,** wife of Dee Waters, first believer in mountains, mother of Jody, Jobe, and Doo Boo

**Mrs. Note** in Striped Creek, Headman Note's wife, mother of Dee Keng and Tu

**Mrs. Pot,** believing daughter-in-law of Mr. and Mrs. Gawk; her husband was an opium addict

**Muti,** Karen Christian worker in Sop Lan, Bible College graduate

**Nang Dee and Bite Gahng,** first Christian couple to get married

**Nang Mung** in Striped Creek, sister to Dee Keng, married to Jo Po

**Old Monday,** headman and demon priest of Hill Village on the plains, father of Abel and Louie

**Shway,** Sgaw Karen evangelist who came to Sandy Creek

**Son Gleck,** Beng Vang's crippled son in Dusty Village

**Song Paw,** from Prosperity Fields, who became a Christian and whose family got sick

**Tu** from Striped Creek, Dee Keng's brother, Bible School graduate, church leader in Striped Creek

**U Vang,** Christian from Buffalo Village whose fields were cursed and children were dying

**White Star,** Mrs. Bite's daughter from Prosperity Fields who believed and then suddenly died